# CLIENT SEDUCTION

## A Step-by-Step Lead Generation System for Professional and Technology Service Firms

by

### Henry DeVries, MBA and
### Denise Bryson, MA

authorHOUSE

*1663 LIBERTY DRIVE, SUITE 200*
*BLOOMINGTON, INDIANA 47403*
*(800) 839-8640*
*www.authorhouse.com*

*First published by AuthorHouse 10/14/04*

*ISBN: 1-4184-0693-7 (e)*
*ISBN: 1-4184-4480-4 (sc)*

*Printed in the United States of America*
*Bloomington, Indiana*

*This book is printed on acid-free paper.*

# Praise for Client Seduction

"The authors expose the myths that often cripple well intended marketing efforts and provide a step-by-step approach to strengthening your 'Client Seduction' plan. A practical reference every IT services executive should read."
Michael R. Thomas, Vice President Strategic Partners—Unisys

"Client Seduction will help you attract more prospects and generate more business than ever before. Read this one over and over, and refer to it again and again."
Mark LeBlanc, author of *Growing Your Business!*

"Client Seduction will shorten significantly your learning curve on how you could get and keep clients. This book is packed with research- and experience-driven lessons useful for anyone who provides professional services."
Glen Broom, Ph.D., professor of communication at San Diego State University, and co-author of *Effective Public Relations*

"Client Seduction is indeed an alluring process to attract prospects cost-effectively and rapidly. This is an ideal resource for the entrepreneur beginning any type of professional services firm."
Alan Weiss, Ph.D., author of *Million Dollar Consulting*

# Table of Contents

# Dedication

This book is dedicated to Dr. Glen Broom and Dr. David Maister

# Chapter 1 : The Good Work Myth

## Being Good Isn't Good Enough

Why are typical marketing and selling practices colossal wastes of time and money for professional and technology service firms? What really works?

Have you heard of The Good Work Myth?

## If you do good work, clients will find you.

That's a common misconception. A four-year best practices study, conducted by the New Client Marketing Institute, proves that statement is pure bunk.

In today's market, it is not enough to offer a great professional or technology service. You must also be able to market and sell your services effectively, which means learning the subtle art of Client Seduction®. And there is a way to have a pipeline filled with leads that are qualified, plentiful, and intensely interested in how you can help them.

Our Client Seduction® system is not about trickery or manipulation; it's about wooing and winning clients by giving away valuable information that helps them solve problems. The more prospects you tell how to solve their problems in general, the more will hire you to apply it to their specific situation.

You want to make it easy and attractive for prospective clients to start dancing with you now and see if romance develops later. This book outlines the step-by-step lead generation system that can help you continually attract enough qualified prospects for your firm to grow and thrive. Begin today, and take persistent action toward your goal of creating a lead generation system.

1

# Chapter 2 : Start With A Guarantee

## Are You Ordinary Or Extraordinary? Prove It!

The Sears catalog built its reputation on it. Rolls Royce has become legendary by offering it. Federal Express transformed it from a begrudging obligation to a powerful marketing tool.

What is it? The extraordinary guarantee. And it just might be the key to substantially increasing your ability to win clients. The vast majority of professional and technology service firms, however, do not and will not guarantee client satisfaction. Why?

## Risk…And Potential

Many of the more than 500 professionals and technology executives interviewed for our lead generation best practices study often shared their own "client from hell" stories when the subject of offering guarantees came up. Professional and technology service firms generally perceive unwarranted risk in offering an extraordinary guarantee. Especially when they offer high-ticket services to a relatively small number of clients, even one client asking for their money back could be painful. And so, they refuse to guarantee their work. (As one humorist noted, sometimes the road less traveled is less traveled for a reason.)

One important book that should have changed the field of professional and technology service firms (but hasn't, yet) is *Extraordinary Guarantees* by Christopher Hart, a former Harvard Business School professor and now president of a quality consulting firm. Hart's first effort to explain the value of guarantees was his 1988 Harvard Business

Review article, "The Power of Unconditional Service Guarantees," which won the prestigious McKinsey Award for "Article of the Year."

Hart's book is a real eye opener. This is not just about Marriott Hotels and Domino's Pizza. In the book, Hart reveals why service companies, which now account for 80 percent of the gross national product, have the greatest opportunity to differentiate themselves through offering a guarantee. He makes a strong case that extraordinary guarantees should be widespread for such professional service firms and technology companies as law offices, management consultancies, advertising agencies, software developers, information technology companies, and even investment bankers.

"But there are reasons why guarantees can also be of exceptional benefit to these firms, especially in winning business of first-time buyers," says Hart. An extraordinary guarantee, well designed and implemented, actually reduces risk and creates value for clients, and this is key when fees can sometimes run into the six figures. When a firm knows that its fees are on the line, commitment to service quality increases—a development that benefits everybody.

"The greater the client's expected aggravation, expense, and time lost, the greater the power of the guarantee," says Hart. As he points out, while bad service at a restaurant can ruin your evening, bad service from a law firm can ruin your life.

Most firms are afraid to offer complete satisfaction. So, a strong guarantee can be the differentiator that makes you stand out in the client's mind.

But how do you make this work in practice? Find a way to fit the concept of a satisfaction guarantee into your own organization. What will you guarantee? Results? Process? On-time delivery? How will satisfaction be measured? At the end of the engagement? Monthly? Quarterly? Examining these questions thoroughly will do two things simultaneously: Allow you to re-engineer your own business to improve performance and ensure client satisfaction, and close more first-time clients by lowering their barriers and perception of risk.

## Making It Work

Here are several examples of professional service firms and technology companies that differentiate themselves by offering clients satisfaction through extraordinary guarantees.

1.  Bain & Company, a global leader in strategy consulting, with more than 2,700 employees in 20 countries, offers some clients an unconditional guarantee on its consulting services. One client was quoted in the *New York Times* as saying: "If they fall short of performance, they don't get paid. Period."

2. Diversified Exchange Corporation, a 1031-exchange company based in La Jolla, prides itself in providing its clients and their advisors with precision performance. They stand behind that with a 100% Performance Guarantee. If a client is not satisfied for any reason, they can directly contact the president, William Exeter, and request a full and complete no-hassles refund of their account set-up fee.

3. Marketing guru Jay Abraham says that "one of the biggest competitive-edge advantages you'll ever gain is always to make it easier for the client to say yes than it is for them to say no." Abraham devotes an entire chapter to extraordinary guarantees in his book, *Getting Everything You Can Out of All You've Got*. An Abraham-trained management consultant agrees, in writing, not to cash any checks he's received until his clients tell him they're satisfied with the work he's done. Another example is the architect who offers a simple pledge: If his client isn't happy at any stage of the project, the architect will refund previously paid fees and re-perform the unsatisfactory work—for free.

4. Author, professional speaker and small business consultant Mark LeBlanc offers participants who attend his weekend Achievers' Circle workshops a remarkable guarantee. There is no set fee for attending the three-day workshop, including all tools and materials. His Web site explains: "At the end of the weekend, we will pass the hat and you will be invited to make a contribution based on the value you have received during the weekend as it relates to the impact on your business and your life." No other products or services are pitched at the seminar. LeBlanc trusts in the participants ability to discern a value and will gratefully accept what they are willing to offer. Does it work? He has held the seminar more than two dozen times.

# When Things Go Wrong, Though…

Before you commit to a guarantee, be sure you understand what you're getting into.

In the final weeks of 2001, two young men were denied their "Guaranteed" rooms at a national hotel chain affiliate in Dallas. The complaint they composed—not a letter, but a very funny PowerPoint show—circled the globe in e-mail chains in just a matter of weeks. By January of 2002, *The Wall Street Journal* had featured the presentation in a story.

We would love to reproduce the slide show for you here, but the authors themselves begged that the proliferation of their slideshow ("Yours is a Very Bad Hotel") be stopped. They've been quoted as saying, "We've had numerous requests to save and show the presentation to business school students, hotel and airline trainees, etc. as an example of customer relations gone horribly wrong. OK, but we have two requirements: please go into the file and alter, "X" out, or delete the names of the managers that appear on the first page... and our e-mail address, which appears on the last page. We are beginning to think that even Night Clerk Mike and his bosses may have suffered enough — and don't deserve to be forever synonymous with bad service. Also, we're already getting more e-mail than we can handle gracefully. Thanks."

We honor their request in this book, but we also think the lesson and entertainment value are worth the effort of finding the original presentation. So, you can read the whole story at http://www.snopes.com/business/consumer/badhotel.asp, and a little bit of creative Googling should yield an archived copy of the PowerPoint.

The moral of the story: If you're going to offer a guarantee, you'd better let all of your employees—even the equivalents of Night Clerk Mike—know what it means to make a guarantee and to honor it—no hassles, no exceptions.

## Five-Step Differentiation Worksheet

You should think in terms of your business plan when you're working out what's unique and different about your business. To that end, review the following questions and be able to answer them in depth.

1. **Overview**

- What is your company's strategic objective? How big would you like to be? What level of revenues? By when?

_____

_____

_____

_____

_____

_____

_____

- Company strategic purpose (why do you exist?)

_____

_____

_____

_____

_____

_____

_____

- Unique selling proposition (what is the difference?)

_____

_____

_____

_____

_____

_____

- Company story (what is your reason for being?)

_____

_____

_____

_____

_____

_____

2. **Growth Plan**

• What are your growth goals?

_____

_____

_____

_____

_____

_____

_____

• What are your assumptions? (i.e., rate of growth, period of time, capital required, operations adjustments needed, etc.)

_____

_____

_____

_____

_____

_____

_____

• Timetable

_____

_____

_____

_____

_____

_____

_____

3. **Management**
- Management goals

_____
_____
_____
_____
_____
_____
_____
_____

- Organizational strategy

_____
_____
_____
_____
_____
_____
_____
_____

- Management team

_____
_____
_____
_____
_____
_____
_____
_____

- Personnel staffing plan

_____

_____

_____

_____

_____

_____

_____

4. **Marketing/Brand**
- Marketing goals

_____

_____

_____

_____

_____

_____

_____

- Overall description of market

_____

_____

_____

_____

_____

_____

_____

- Brand positioning and image strategy

_____
_____
_____
_____
_____
_____
_____

- Target market descriptions

_____
_____
_____
_____
_____
_____
_____

5. **Customer Satisfaction Plan**
- Customer satisfaction goals

_____
_____
_____
_____
_____
_____
_____

- Products/services descriptions

_____

_____

_____

_____

_____

_____

_____

- Production strategy

_____

_____

_____

_____

_____

_____

_____

- Service strategy

_____

_____

_____

_____

_____

_____

_____

- Delivery strategy

_____

_____

_____

_____

_____

_____

_____

_____

- Customer service strategy

_____

_____

_____

_____

_____

_____

_____

Once you've assembled all of the information above and can see "The big picture," work to boil it all down to what makes you DIFFERENT from everybody else out there who does what you do. One sentence is the ultimate goal, although you may not get there for a while.

# Deliverable

The Promise. Start drafting your unique selling proposition. In this step, you concentrate on your business—you decide who you are, what you do, and what makes you different from everybody else.

<u><Our firm></u> is a <u><specialized description></u> specializing in <services provided>. Unlike <u>typical <generic company label></u>, we use a proprietary process and offer a 100% satisfaction guarantee.

# Examples

- <Firm X> is an information technology professional services firm that focuses on using Microsoft.NET for e-business application development and integration. As opposed to software resellers...

- Welcome to <Firm Y>, your partner in troubleshooting, networking and technical support. Unlike other computer consultants...

# Chapter 3 : Identify Your Target Market

## How Can You Narrow Your Focus?

Before you can generate solid leads, you need to define, clearly and succinctly, your business. What kind of business are you? What do you do? For whom? What makes your services different from all the other providers out there?

You must also decide to target a market niche that will be profitable. In today's market, clients demand specialists. You want fewer prospects to be interested in you, but much more intensely interested.

Developing a plan to promote your business to a target market takes time, effort, and a dedication that most new entrepreneurs, or busy established businesses, think they don't have. It's important to identify the target audience, or the customers you intend to reach. Provide specific information about the people your company considers its clients. It's also important to identify user trends, or those changes in the market that can create opportunities for your company.

1. Are you interested in solving the problems they have?
2. Do they know you already?
3. Can they afford you?
4. Are they willing to pay more for better service?
5. Do they already know they need you?
6. Are they numerous?
7. Do you have few real competitors with this audience?
8. Can you find them (lists, etc.)?
9. Are there enough of them in your easy-travel region?
10. Are they going to be great flagship clients and references?

You'll need some type of research to complete your plan, but have no fear—plenty is available. Secondary research is broad research that has been conducted by others, and is found at libraries and on Internet Web sites. Take advantage of it.

## Low-Cost And No-Cost Ways To Use The Internet To Gather Competitive Intelligence

Before our firm undertakes a marketing plan or a public relations campaign, we conduct an analytical research study of a company's industry and competition. Here are some other low-cost and no-cost ways to search.

**Gentlemen, start your search engines.** There are only about 1,800 to choose from. Our two favorites are the super fast Google (google.com) and Go (go.com), which lets you do searches within searches. Of course, every search begins by going to the Web sites of competing businesses. Then we search by topic. Don't forget to use different words and phrases. Some of the other popular search engines are:


- Alta Vista (altavista.com)
- Excite (excite.com)
- HotBot (hotbot.com)
- Infoseek (infoseek.com)
- Lycos (lycos.com)
- MSN Search (searchmsn.com)
- Open Directory (dmoz.org)
- Yahoo! (yahoo.com)


- **Go where the writers go.** Check out the reference links at the Writer's Guild of America Web site (wga.org). This is a great portal to a number of online databases, encyclopedias and directories.
- **Get to know university librarians.** Because Universities have business schools, the library has invested in many online databases. By doing your research at the university's library you can have free access to many research databases that would normally charge. We recommend starting your search for trade magazine articles with RDS/Business & Industry, Lexis-Nexis Academic Universe and Dow-Jones Interactive. You can either pay to print out the information or e-mail it to yourself. Speaking of college libraries, try the Simon Fraser University Library "Business Marketing Research" page (lib.sfu.ca/kiosk/mbodnar/market.html).
- **Visit the Electronic Library.** While RDS/Business & Industry will get you the trade articles, the elibrary.com Web site is a great place to get access to the

consumer media. This database includes thousands of full-text newspapers, magazines, television, book and photo archives. You can take advantage of the free trial subscription for starters. You can search for up to 150 articles on any given subject.

- **All the news that's fit to sell.** *The New York Times* (nytimes.com), *The Wall Street Journal* (wsj.com) and the *San Jose Mercury News* (sjmercury.com) all have great story archives. The search and headlines are free, but a download of the article will cost you. For business magazines, I prefer *Inc.* (inc.com) and *Forbes* (forbes.com), which both let you search the archives and print articles for free.
- **Go see your analyst.** Don't have thousands of dollars to spend on an industry analyst study? There is a cheaper way. Check the news releases on the industry analyst sites for appropriate statistics. Here are some of the best places to go for information technology stuff.

  - GartnerGroup
  - Yankee Group
  - Meta Group
  - IDG
  - Forrester Research
  - Jupiter Communications
  - Dataquest
  - EStats.com

- **Shop the competition.** Do you know what a mystery shopper is? That's one of those people hired to pretend to shop at a store to monitor the customer's experience. If possible, you should try to do the same. If practical, actually buy something.
- **You have my permission.** Permission Marketing is currently in vogue. Does the competitive company have an opt-in e-mail invitation on its Web site? By all means, give them your e-mail to see what you will receive.
- **At your wire services.** We like both Business Wire (businesswire.com) and PR Newswire (prnewswire.com). These provide electronic delivery of news releases and information from companies. For financial news also try Dow Jones Newswires (dowjones.com/newswires), Reuters (reuters.com) and Bloomberg (bloomberg.com).

Here's a grid example of how to work out these questions with various target audiences.

| Criterion | Butchers | Bakers | Candlestick Makers | Surfers |
|---|---|---|---|---|
| Money? | ☐Yes ☐No | ☐Yes ☐No | ☐Yes ☐No | ☐Yes ☐No |
| Premium payers? | ☐Yes ☐No | ☐Yes ☐No | ☐Yes ☐No | ☐Yes ☐No |
| Numerous? | ☐Yes ☐No | ☐Yes ☐No | ☐Yes ☐No | ☐Yes ☐No |
| Weak competition? | ☐Yes ☐No | ☐Yes ☐No | ☐Yes ☐No | ☐Yes ☐No |
| Lists available? | ☐Yes ☐No | ☐Yes ☐No | ☐Yes ☐No | ☐Yes ☐No |
| Expertise in the field? | ☐Yes ☐No | ☐Yes ☐No | ☐Yes ☐No | ☐Yes ☐No |
| Are you interested? | ☐Yes ☐No | ☐Yes ☐No | ☐Yes ☐No | ☐Yes ☐No |
| Do they already know they need you? | ☐Yes ☐No | ☐Yes ☐No | ☐Yes ☐No | ☐Yes ☐No |
| Close to you or within geographic range? | ☐Yes ☐No | ☐Yes ☐No | ☐Yes ☐No | ☐Yes ☐No |
| Good reference potential? | ☐Yes ☐No | ☐Yes ☐No | ☐Yes ☐No | ☐Yes ☐No |

Obviously, those potential client pools who accumulate the most checks in the "Yes" column are keepers—focus on no more than three in the first year, preferably ONE. Now, add your target market to your developing positioning statement. Remember, you're defining who you are, down to the smallest detail. You can't be all things to all people. They don't want you to be. People trust specialists, not generalists. They will hire you when they believe you have the knowledge and the experience to work with them, specifically.

## Examples

1. Welcome to <Firm Y>, your partner in troubleshooting, networking and technical support. We work with architects, attorneys, and providers of complementary healthcare to streamline their information technology systems and provide total, end-to-end support.
2. Welcome to <Firm Z>, a strategic partner providing professional, executive management services for businesses in transition with revenues of $10-50M. Unlike other management consultants, we employ an analysis and planning process developed over a 30-year period. The Comprehensive Business Review™ assesses your firm's strengths and vulnerabilities in six foundational arenas. A one-of-a-kind plan emerges from this process, offering you a highly tailored set of strategies and tactics to strengthen and optimize each facet of your business.

> ## Deliverable
>
> Positioning. Continue to draft your unique selling proposition. Here, you insert your target market niches. This version will read much like the following.
>
> <Our firm> is a <specialized description> specializing in <services provided> for , , and companies. Unlike typical <generic company label>, we use a proprietary process and offer a 100% satisfaction guarantee.

Here's a blank worksheet to use as you think about narrowing your focus.

Who are your three top target markets? Fill them into the following grid, then answer "Yes" or "No" to each "Ideal Target Qualifier." This grid can help you to prioritize which market to target FIRST—and you may need to shape your message specifically for each target market.)

| Qualifying Question | Target 1 | Target 2 | Target 3 |
|---|---|---|---|
| Do they have problems you can solve? | ☐ | ☐ | ☐ |
| Do they know they have the problem? | ☐ | ☐ | ☐ |
| Are they able and willing to pay to solve the problem? | ☐ | ☐ | ☐ |
| Are there a lot of them? | ☐ | ☐ | ☐ |
| Is there enough "room" in your space to be competitive? (i.e., there's no 800-pound gorilla out there dominating the market) | ☐ | ☐ | ☐ |
| Can you buy lists to help you reach them? | ☐ | ☐ | ☐ |
| Have you already established credibility with businesses like them? | ☐ | ☐ | ☐ |
| Do their issues interest you? | ☐ | ☐ | ☐ |
| Are they geographically desirable? | ☐ | ☐ | ☐ |
| Will they make good references? | ☐ | ☐ | ☐ |

# Chapter 4 : Name The Pain

## Why Do Clients Come To You? What Problems Do They Have That You Can Solve?

You need to be able to tell people why your clients hire you every day—at networking events, on sales calls, at lunch when you meet somebody new. In this Chapter, you'll create a three-point "elevator" speech that calls out the three most acute pains that you can solve for potential clients.

Prospects will become clients for one reason and one reason only: They have pain.

In this Chapter, you will think about the most common problems your clients have. List them all, no matter how big or how small. Look at your list and see if there are any patterns. How can you sum up the three biggest pains you solve?

## Pain Worksheet

List every single thing that worries, frustrates, or concerns your chosen target market. But try to keep it at the level of things that will keep your prospect awake at night. "Their current vendors don't meet deadlines" isn't a pain yet, because there aren't any personal, agonizing, anxiety-producing consequences in that statement. On the other hand, "I'm worried I'll lose my job or the company will go bankrupt because we hire the wrong vendor and they won't meet the deadline" is a *serious pain*. See the difference?

_____

_____

_____

_____

_____

_____

_____

_____

_____

_____

_____

_____

_____

Now, go back to what you've just written. CIRCLE the worries, concerns, and frustrations that YOU CAN FIX.

Finally, UNDERLINE the circled items that ONLY you can fix—nobody else. (If there aren't any just yet, think about how you can refine or rephrase the circled items to make your firm the best answer).

Choose the best three pains you've come up with and add them to the beginnings of your elevator speech. There. You've done it. You've positioned yourself!

## Deliverable

1. **Your Pain Proposition.** When you speak with people, you will deliver the pain proposition immediately after your Unique Selling Proposition. You may also use it in print—on paper or online. It's the hook you dangle to get potential clients to bite.

You'll eventually put the three most common pains into emotional language that motivates people to want to solve them. Words like "Frustrated," "Worried," "Concerned," "Upset about," and so on, help to set this tone. When you combine the pain proposition with the pains, you've arrived at a positioning statement (sometimes called a "20-second commercial." You should strive to memorize it and use it as often as you possibly can.

**Typically, clients hire us because they're...**

---

Frustrated about...<u><pain 1></u>
Worried that...<pain 2>
Concerned that...<pain 3>

2. **Your Completed 20-second commercial.** Now, put it all together. Learn it. Memorize it. Live it. Breathe it. Slip it into everyday conversation. Repeat it until telling people exactly who you are and what you do is second nature.
<u><Our firm></u> is a <u><specialized description></u> specializing in <services provided> for <u></u>, <u></u>, and <u></u> companies. Unlike <u>typical <generic company label></u>, we use a proprietary process and offer a 100% satisfaction guarantee.
Typically, when I speak with business owners—someone like yourself— they tell me they're frustrated with <u><pain 1></u>, worried about <u><pain 2></u>, or concerned about <u><pain 3></u>. But I don't suppose you have any of those problems...

# Chapter 5 : Check Your Reflection

## Do Your Tangibles Communicate A First-Class Image?

There are five attributes that clients use to judge professionals, and appealing tangibles heads the list. Tangibles include anything physical that will affect a potential client's perception of you and your company. This is where it pays to overspend. You never get a second chance to make a first impression.

Your tangibles include a multitude of concrete, material items. Your workspace, your wardrobe, your personal grooming. Your furniture, the art on your business's walls. Your business cards, the look and feel of your web sites and e-mails. Your company colors. Your handouts, copies, faxes, brochures. Everything.

Many thanks to Chris Cavanaugh, President of The Christopher Company, for his insights on logos. You can find examples of The Christopher Company's work, more information about the company and free design resources at www.christophercompany.com.

## 5 Reasons Why A Logo Is An Important Part Of Your Marketing

1. A logo differentiates your business from others visually, identifying the product or service you provide.
2. It creates a sweet spot, a point of familiarity between you and the marketplace.
3. It should exude authenticity. Customers crave what's real and genuine. A logo that looks like clip art demeans your business.
4. A good logo builds your brand. It's your promise to perform. And a promise is the heart of good advertising.

5.  A logo is one of the most valuable assets of your business. The more it's used, the more equity it builds. And the more image and brand equity you have, the more valuable your business becomes. This is especially important if you plan to someday sell your company.

# 7 Problems To Avoid When Designing Your Logo

1.  **Avoid using too thin a line weight.** Thin lines can disappear or break up in some publications.
2.  **Keep your logo simple and meaningful.** If it's too abstract many people won't understand it.
3.  **Keep it balanced and in proportion.** A logo designed in the wrong proportions for most applications will seem amateurish.
4.  **Stay away from fad typefaces that will soon be old-fashioned.**
5.  **Steer clear of the obvious because it's probably overused.** Resorting to visual clichés makes people think you're a cliché.
6.  **Putting a rectangular box around a series of letters** is not very imaginative and could hardly be called a logo design.
7.  **Just because a logo is attractive doesn't mean it's effective.** If it doesn't convey information about your business, it's not serving its purpose.

# 5 Characteristics Of A Good Logo Design

1.  **An effective logo looks good small as well as large.** It should have the same visual effect when printed on a business card or a billboard.
2.  **A good logo does not rely on color to be effective.** Many times you can only use the logo in one color, such as in faxing or in the newspaper. That's one of the reasons why this guide is in black and white. It shows the logos in their purest form.
3.  **A good logo has a visual 'hook' that is appealing to the eye.** Its unique design suggests that your business is also unique.
4.  **Ideally a logo should avoid using screens or graduated ink.** In printing terms, a screen is a tint of one ink that makes it look lighter than the color at 100% value. In using a 50% screen, for example, the printed result appears half as dark. Screens are difficult to reproduce clearly and consistently.
5.  **An effective logo is simple rather than complex.** Too many elements, or a logo that is too detailed or too complex reduces recognition and legibility, especially at smaller sizes. Express the idea about your company as simply, clearly and directly as possible.

# Marketing Experts Comment About The Benefits Of A Business Identity

"A logo is a visual representation of your company. This should look good at any size. A logo is a very important choice to make and should never be changed once you've decided upon a good one. Two million businesses are formed each year, and a logo will help you stand out from these."

Jay Conrad Levinson, *Guerrilla Marketing,* Houghton Mifflin, Boston, 1984

"Be careful to present yourself so that others' first impressions correspond to what you want . . . Wear your facade with pride."

Richard Koch, *The Natural Laws of Business,* Doubleday, New York, 2000

"Realize that your company is going to project an image regardless of whether you plan it or not. That image is either going to help or hurt you."

Richard White, *The Entrepreneur's Manual,* Chilton Book Co., Radnor, PA, 1977

# Logo Design Process

How much time is spent on a logo depends on your needs. In all cases, there are a number of stages we go through to create your logo design.

## Objective Meeting

What is your company's personality? Who are your customers? How do they think of your company? How would you like to be perceived? What is your principle product or service and what are its benefits? All this is drawn out during the objective meeting and taken into consideration. The amount of time spent in these meetings will vary. While one logo might require only a 15-minute phone call, another may require a site visit.

## Determine the Type of Logo

Logo styles need to be considered and narrowed down to one or two types.

## Concept Development

The term "Think outside the Box" is used often but rarely understood. "The Box" is the limitation that designers place on themselves when they go with their first instinct or use someone else's less qualified opinion. Although the first idea could be the best, this cannot be known until other ideas are explored.

## Thumbnail Sketches

Once an idea is formulated, the designer will generate a number of thumbnail sketches. The point of this Chapter is to get as many ideas on paper as possible without getting hung up on any particular one.

## Roughs

The designer picks the best ideas and brings them to a point where they can be presented. This could be done on paper, at the computer or both.

## Refinement

The roughs undergo revision so the quality is polished to perfection.

## Illustration

Often a logo involves the use of an illustration, which, in many cases, is created from scratch.

## Typography

Typography includes manipulation of characters such as leading and kerning, and sometimes even the creation of a typeface. Each has a subtle effect on the quality, aesthetics and readability of the type. Beyond the basics, the characters of the type might be manipulated to create your own unique version of a typeface. If the type is integrated to form a picture, the typography can become a creative illustration in itself.

## Presentation

A person-to-person presentation can help us quickly narrow logo choices, as we work to identify which design elements work best. We try to distinguish the scientific from the subjective by focusing on each element of the logo separately.

## Symbol Selection

Examining the symbols alone–without accompanying type–can help determine its effectiveness as part of the logo. Nike's and Apple's corporate symbols have enough recognition to be used without the company names. If the symbol alone creates enough interest or recognition, then we're on the right track.

## Symbol Refinement & Style Application

Once a symbol is chosen, it's a good idea to explore different illustration styles to match the desired personality of the company. This Chapter also serves as the client's last chance to identify any features they find problematic. It's easier to be critical at this stage than later on.

## Type Selection

Once the symbol and the illustration style are chosen, a typeface should be selected to complement the style of the symbol.

## Type Refinement & Arrangement

The arrangement of a logo's elements will determine the overall shape of the logo and is an integral part of the overall design. While one company might have more use for a horizontal shaped logo, another may be better served by a vertical shape.

## Color Studies & Selection

Even though logos should be effective in black & white, it's helpful to explore which colors work best with your new logo. This Chapter allows the client to see how well the logo works with a particular color or a variety of colors. This Chapter is saved for last because it is very easy to change the color of a logo.

## Logo Delivery

We deliver the logo in both printed and electronic form—in the most common format for professional use. Most computer applications can import EPS vector files. Both the electronic files and stats print are delivered in a folder with detailed explanations. Here are some examples of "before and after" transformations that Cavanaugh provided, with his commentary.

| BEFORE | AFTER |
|---|---|
|  ESCONDIDO COMMUNITY HEALTH CENTER |  NEIGHBORHOOD HEALTHCARE |

| | |
|---|---|
| Strictly clip art trying to decorate type. The main problems here are that the lines and triangles add nothing to the copy. And the name is set in a difficult to read, dated font. | They ended up with an icon that is meant to suggest a figure jumping as well as the hills and sun over the inland areas where this chain of clinics is located. The name font was rendered more legible and contemporary. |

| | |
|---|---|
|  |  |

| | |
|---|---|
| The use of a box around a clip art image of a bottle of wine, a glass and some grapes suggest wine appreciation. It does not relate to the core skill of the company, which is building custom wine cellars. | The use of the V hints at a wine cellar rack while the highlight circle on the bottom of the bottles suggests the C in Cellars. Together they both define the letters of the company and indicate what the company does. |

| | |
|---|---|
| JONES SURPLUS WE BUY AND SELL QUALITY CATV EQUIPMENT |  BROADBAND INTERNATIONAL |

| | |
|---|---|
| The thumbs-up clip art graphic was perhaps intended to indicate that the company is A-Ok or that their products are a "go". This did not relate at all to what the company does. There was an attempt to give it a "look" with the use of the horizontal lines and the dual use of the S in Jones to work into both the name and the word surplus. | The company re-oriented itself towards fiber-optics. The dominant element became the stylized J which cuts through all the letters in the name and ends in a starburst in the last letter. The balance of the name is nested below and balances out the name and mark. |

# Homework

Review, revise and, if necessary refine or redesign the most important of your existing tangibles.

- Logo
- Business Cards
- Stationery
- Office furniture
- Walls and décor
- Wardrobe
- Look and feel of printed materials
- Snacks
- What else?

Consider the impression a stranger might have if she walked in the door for the first time and saw your tangibles.

Tangibles are everything you can see, hear, smell, taste, and touch. It's not just your logo and color scheme, stationery, letterhead, and business cards; it's also your signs, office space, furniture arrangement, accessories, décor, employee dress, demeanor, answering machine message…even the candy bowl at the reception desk.

What's working? What's not? What could be improved? How quickly? Do your tangibles say "Trust Me"?

## Deliverable

Start planning now to optimize your tangibles. You may not have the budget right now to reprint all of your collateral, but put it on your list. Meanwhile, could you change the greeting on your voice-mail? Add a bunch of fresh flowers from a local farmer's market to your reception area? Drop into the warehouse center and stock up on healthy snacks and an attractive dish to put them in?

Create a comprehensive assessment of all your tangibles. Some people might want to keep track of their findings in a database or spreadsheet; others may find a simple checklist is enough to get the ball rolling. If you find it helpful, you can use the following format.

## Tangibles Plan

Item: LOGO & Visual Identity

Status:      ☐Matches ideal image            ☐Needs Improvement

Improvement Needed:     _____

Target Completion Date:     _____

Item: Stationery, Cards, Envelopes

Status:      ☐Matches ideal image            ☐Needs Improvement

Improvement Needed:     _____

Target Completion Date:     _____

Item: Office Space (Building, walls)

Status: □Matches ideal image   □Needs Improvement

Improvement Needed:  _____

Target Completion Date:  _____

Item: Office Decor (furniture, carpets, lighting, color, flowers, artwork...)

Status: □Matches ideal image   □Needs Improvement

Improvement Needed:  _____

Target Completion Date:  _____

Item: Image Folder (See Chapter 9)

Status: □Matches ideal image   □Needs Improvement

Improvement Needed:  _____

Target Completion Date:  _____

Item: Employee Physical Appearance

Status: □Matches ideal image   □Needs Improvement

Improvement Needed:  _____

Target Completion Date:  _____

Item: Vehicles (if applicable)

Status:          □Matches ideal image                    □Needs Improvement

Improvement Needed:          _____

Target Completion Date:          _____

Item: Printed materials (if applicable)

Status:          □Matches ideal image                    □Needs Improvement

Improvement Needed:          _____

Target Completion Date:          _____

Item: Products and Packaging (if applicable)

Status:          □Matches ideal image                    □Needs Improvement

Improvement Needed:          _____

Target Completion Date:          _____

Item: Other

Status:          □Matches ideal image                    □Needs Improvement

Improvement Needed:          _____

Target Completion Date:          _____

# Chapter 6 : Formalize Your Proprietary Process

## What Could Your Proprietary Process Be?
## What Would You Name It?

You gain enormous leverage when you formalize something you've probably already got: A proprietary problem-solving process that you will now name and protect by obtaining a trademark.

Your process should have an enigmatic name that prompts questions; you want to be asked to explain it.

A proprietary process is not only a marketing asset that will allow you to charge more, but also will make your work less accidental and improve the quality of your service.

## How To Win Clients With A Proprietary Process

When potential clients tell you their problems, they expect you to tell them how you can solve them. This is the moment of truth: The time you explain how you solve problems like theirs. After you suggest a solution, you want them thinking, "At last... someone who understands my problem and really knows what they are doing."

There's an old marketing saying that goes like this: "If you don't have anything unique to advertise about your business, then you should advertise your business for sale." To woo and win clients, you need a distinct problem-solving methodology for your professional service firm or technology-based service company. This is your proprietary process, an approach unique to your firm.

As of February 2004, a Google search on "proprietary process" yielded more than 29,000 hits. This represents more than a doubling in fewer than six months (October 2003 resulted in only 13,000 hits). Obviously, the proprietary process, as a marketing technique, is gaining currency in the marketplace.

Nashville-based business consultant David Baker says one of the most common mistakes a professional service firm can make is not having a defined, proprietary process. Writing in his newsletter *Persuading* (available through his Web site, www. recourses.com), Baker highlights several reasons why a proprietary process is important.

"Process is differentiating, highlighting the uniqueness of your firm with a process that you own," says Baker. Other advantages he cites are that a process demonstrates your experience, makes your work less accidental and will even allow you to charge more. "Clients are always willing to pay more for packages than individual hours within a fee structure."

A good proprietary process, however, is never a cut-and-dried industry standard lifted from a textbook. Instead, it codifies a firm's particular method of problem-solving, typically identifying and sequencing multiple steps that often take place in the same, defined order. Furthermore, the completed process should have an intriguing name—one that you can trademark.

What are some of these intriguing proprietary process names? Here are a few to ponder:
- The I-Innovation Process™
- The SupporTrak RACE System™
- The NetRaker Methodology™
- The Systematic Determination Process™
- The Persuasion Iteration Process®
- The Innovation Continuum Methodology™

Don't worry if you don't understand what any of these processes do just by hearing the names: That's actually the point.

A name that is unique enough to actually qualify to be trademarked will also create the opportunity to explain the process to potential clients.

Don't go overboard, however, and create a name that is all marketing hype with no real service substance. Sometimes a line from a movie says it all. Remember when every burger joint had a secret sauce? In the film "Fast Times at Ridgemont High," teenage workers from various fast food restaurants reveal what goes into the "secret sauce" for their hamburgers. One says "ketchup and mayonnaise," and the other says "Thousand Island dressing."

Make sure that some real problem-solving ingredients have gone into the secret sauce of your firm—your proprietary process—and that the name actually reflects your unique approach.

## Let It Flow

Most clients are attracted by specialization first, and then by a proprietary process. Here are some recommendations to create your own defined problem-solving system that will help you attract clients.

Outline what you already do to solve client problems

↓

Break this process down into a series of defined steps
(usually from five to seven are enough)

↓

Give the process an intriguing name, typically no more than four words. Begin with
"The" and ending with "System," "Process," or "Methodology"

↓

Search the U.S. Patent Office Web site (www.uspto.gov) to find out whether you can
trademark the name (steer clear if it's already been used in your industry)

↓

Seek legal protection of the process as intellectual property through the U.S. Patent
Office

↓

Include the process on your Web site, but only give enough detail to describe it in
general, so you have room to adapt it for each selling situation

↓

Continually improve the process, and be sure to document the improvements

## Create An Internal Blueprint

In addition to the process documentation you show your clients, you should have a detailed internal document on how you use the proprietary process. The truism about service businesses is that people come and go, but the process is forever.

According to Professor Christopher Lovelock of the Yale Business School, you should create a blueprint of your business's process, a visual map of the sequence of activities required to complete the process for clients. To develop a blueprint, you need first to identify all of the key activities in the service design and production.

Service blueprints clarify the interactions between clients and members of the firm. "This can be beneficial, since operationally oriented businesses are sometimes so focused on managing backstage activities that they neglect to consider the customer's view of front-stage activities," writes Lovelock in his book *Services Marketing*. "Accounting firms, for instance, often have elaborately documented procedures and standards for how to conduct an audit properly, but may lack clear standards for when and how to host a client meeting or how to answer the telephone when clients call."

## How To Trademark Your Proprietary Process

Does what you sell to clients cost more than $1,000? To win clients, you need a distinct problem-solving methodology for your professional service firm, consulting practice or technology-based service company. This is your proprietary process, an approach unique to your firm.

Are you safeguarding your intellectual assets? Protecting physical property – such as buildings and cars – is an obvious choice for most business people because these things are visible and tangible. We can all see it, stand on it or ride in it. But what about trade secrets, trade names and copyrights? Intellectual property is another matter, because it is not easy to see and much harder to value.

Annually the United States issues 100,000 patents, 60,000 trademarks and more than 600,000 copyrights. The system is beautiful to behold when it goes right.

"As an attorney who has helped protect thousands of products and services in the past decade, I also have seen the unfortunate consequences when things go wrong," says attorney Larry Binderow, a specialist in trademarks, copyright protection and domestic/international licensing and franchising. "The stakes are high because counterfeit and fraudulent use of intellectual property costs U.S. business more than $60 billion per year."

When a mark is registered by the United States Patent and Trademark Office, Binderow recommends that notice of the registration be given by placing the familiar "circle-R" ® symbol adjacent to the mark as used on labels or packaging, and in advertising or similar publications.

According to Binderow, it pays to know the proper use of this symbol (or an alternative form of registration notice) with federally registered trademarks, service marks, collective marks and certification marks.

### Reasons for Using a Registration Notice

Display of a registration notice is not mandatory. Use of the notice is recommended, however, for the following reasons:

- The notice advises the public of your claim to exclusive use of the mark on goods or services specified in the registration.
- The notice advises the public that the word or symbol is being used to designate the goods or services of the registration owner, and not merely as an ordinary adjective or product name. The notice also serves as a helpful warning to newspaper or magazine writers to avoid using the mark as a generic term.
- Should an infringement occur, failure to use a registration notice will limit recovery of damages or profits to the period when the infringer was aware of the existence of the registration.

## Acceptable Forms of Registration Notices

The federal trademark laws specify the following three styles of acceptable notices:
1. ®
2. Reg. U.S. Pat. & TM Off.
3. Registered in U.S. Patent and Trademark Office

"I recommend use of the ® symbol because it is short and easy to insert without upsetting the graphic balance of labels, brochures, and other displays of the registered mark," says Bindreow. "Positioning of the notice is not critical, but the ® symbol is normally used as a superscript immediately after the mark. There is no required minimum size for the ® symbol, and a small, unobtrusive size is perfectly acceptable as long as it is legible."

## Points to Check before Using a Registration Notice

Binderow warns that it is improper to use any of the above-listed registration notices with a mark until a federal registration of the mark has been issued. Mere filing of an application for registration does not authorize use of the notice. Similarly, issuance of a state registration does not authorize use of the ® symbol or the other notice forms listed above.

In the interim, a permissible and recommended procedure is to use a™ on trademarks not protected by a federal registration.

---

# Homework

1. **The Process.** Think about the process you use to initiate and complete projects for your clients. Make notes on the steps you already go through. You may find it helpful to try to explain your methods to somebody who doesn't already know what you do. Have them take notes.

You need to break your process down into a particular number of steps, in a particular order. As a general rule, some numbers work better than others.

2. **The Name.** The name of your process should make what you do sound complicated and valuable. Some examples: "The Persuasion Iteration." "The Integrated Differentiation Method." "The Progressive Deconstruction Process."

---

## The Process

You already have a process. It's the way you do things, step by step, from the minute a client engages with you until the work is done. You're going to outline it now.

Only one constraint: At this stage, don't aim for more than 10 steps. Keep it short and simple.

And if you only end up with four steps or five, you're fine, too.

Step 1: We _____

Step 2: We _____

Step 3: We _____

Step 4: We _____

Step 5: We _____

Step 6: We _____

Step 7: We _____

Step 8: We _____

Step 9: We _____

Step 10: We _____

## The Process Name

We think a simple formula will name your process 90% of the time. It's a "Mad Lib" approach.

The _____

System / Process.

Use the space below to come up with words that describe what you do and how. Some combination of them may be your best process name.

One from Column A: How

One from Column B: What

| *Progressive* | *Deconstruction* |
| *Systematic* | *Differentiation* |
| *Iterative* | *Productivity* |
| | |
| | |
| | |
| | |
| | |
| | |
| | |
| | |

## Deliverables

1. A written description of your proprietary process.
2. A unique and enigmatic name for the entire process.
3. Evocative names for each step in the process.
4. <optional> A flowchart or diagram of your process to use in presentations

## Notes

_____

_____

_____

_____

_____

_____

_____

_____

_____

_____

_____

_____

_____

_____

_____

_____

_____

_____

# Chapter 7 : Go Silver, Gold, and Platinum

## Does Your Pricing Strategy Optimize Trust (And Revenue)?

You wouldn't eat at a restaurant that only offered one meal. You wouldn't enroll your children in a college that offers only one major. You wouldn't subscribe to a cable service that has only one channel.

Your clients are no different.

Give them a range of choices. No doubt you offer more than one kind of service or level of service; package these creatively in ways that will let clients feel in control of their buying. We use the terms "Silver," "Gold," and "Platinum" as shorthand; you can name your packages whatever you like, so long as it makes sense and implies a scale of value.

"Silver" packages are the lowest level of service you'll offer—bare-bones, no frills, pragmatic, and no-nonsense. Your Silver package should be the one you currently offer when somebody beats you up to get the lowest price; the lowest you can go and still remain profitable.

"Gold" packages add more features, or frequency, or services; they're the ones most clients will choose, because most people believe moderation is a good thing. A bonus for you, as the provider of services, is that you can charge more at the Gold level than you would have in a straight RFP or one-bid sales process.

Finally, there's your "Platinum" package. This is the package that will attract the kind of client who shops exclusively at Nordstrom and Neiman-Marcus. This package is for the client who likes to say, "I'm worth it." You may not sell a large number of them, but when you do, you'll be satisfied that you didn't leave money on the table.

Finally, it's important that, regardless of which package your new client chooses, it's still guaranteed. If you can't offer a 100% satisfaction guarantee on Silver Package work, consider whether it's worth offering at all. Your reputation is at stake with every client at every level: If you can't afford to do your best work at your lowest price point, then you may need to consider raising your prices.

## An Example

Company X, below, offers custom publicity widgetry.

They offer clients three levels of service.

Which would you choose?

| Platinum: ($15,000) | You get...<br><br>• Basic Services<br>• Tickertape parade<br>• Marching band<br>• Bells<br>• Whistles<br>• Bubble gum |
| --- | --- |
| Gold: ($10,000) | • Basic Services<br>• Bells<br>• Whistles<br>• Bubble gum |
| Silver: ($7,500) | • Basic Services<br>• Whistles |

Most people, faced with such a choice, tend to purchase the middle option. "Bells and whistles are fine, and we don't need a tickertape parade," goes the typical thinking. So, load your Platinum package up to the hilt, and rest assured that most potential clients are like Goldilocks. They don't want too much, or too little. They want to buy "just right."

## Homework

Think about creative ways to package your services to arrive at a tiered service system.

## Deliverable

A one-page description of your services, broken into at least two packages (and preferably three). Feel free to rename the packages to fit your branding, and make sure that everything included in each level of service is spelled out clearly.

# Chapter 8 : (Re)Build Your Web site

## How Can You Build Your Brand Online?

Next, you create an easy-to-update, database-driven Web site that demonstrates your competence, not asserts how great you are.

The Web site is the cornerstone of the new marketing, and must not be a mere electronic brochure.

There are a thousand and one current books available on web design, and a lot of free information available on the web itself. Don't go it alone. Study, research, and make sure that you're designing a site that builds trust—give away lots of good, free information. Don't waste your users' time. Make it easy for them to sign up for newsletters or other free goodies. And think of the site as an investment, not an expense.

## 21 Must-Have Web Site Elements

Your Web site should be the cornerstone of your lead generation efforts. The site is your silent salesperson—the one with whom prospective clients visit before granting you permission to meet with them.

A top priority for any firm that competes in the professional services or technology space is to create an easy-to-update Web site that demonstrates your competence. As the Internet matures, content is slowly becoming more important, but it's amazing how many sites for such firms simply assert how great the company is, rather than helping prospective clients.

If client seduction is defined as the art of wooing and winning clients by giving away valuable information, what are the classic client seduction Web site blunders?

According to our best practices research, the three most common errors are Web sites that are too busy; web sites that feature little more than lengthy company histories and other information important to the company itself; and worst of all, a site devoid of meaningful, useful how-to information. Without how-to information, a Web site is just a glorified electronic brochure.

From a best-practices standpoint, here are 21 must-have elements for a superior Web site that begins the client seduction dance.

1.  **A clear positioning statement.** Tell prospective clients, in as few words as possible, what you do, whom you do it for, and what results you achieve. If you have a proprietary process or an extraordinary guarantee, this is the time and place to mention it.

2.  **Free resources.** The key to earning your prospective clients' trust is to demonstrate that you know how to solve their problems in general. They will hire you to solve specific problems. With that key fact in mind, your Web site should be filled with how-to articles, white papers and special reports that give away valuable information.

3.  **Declare your specialization.** The number one attribute prospective clients hunt for is specialization, so put yours right up front. No successful small firm is "all things to all people;" figure out who you serve, and how, and put that information on the front page. Be sure also to describe the outcomes you achieve, such as decreased costs or increased revenues.

4.  **Mission and philosophy.** According to our focus groups, you should include a mission statement, but keep it short and meaningful. Clients say they don't really care that much about mission statements, but if you can use one to further differentiate yourself, it's a good idea to do so.

5.  **Contact information.** Don't make your prospective clients work to find you. Put your phone number on every page. Make it easy for prospective clients to e-mail you with requests for more information or a meeting. And definitely consolidate all of your contact information on one page, including address, fax numbers, and so on.

6.  **Map and driving directions.** If prospects ever visit your physical location, then you must include a map and driving directions to your office. This will not only save you time, but is also another reason to have prospective clients poking around your Web site.

7.  **E-mail subscription link.** Forrester Research studies show that converting prospects into clients via e-mail is 20 times more cost-effective than using direct mail. Once you capture their e-mail, why waste first-class postage? Offer prospective clients solid reasons for giving you permission to e-mail them; free

reports, studies, white papers, or notifications of key Web site updates. And of course, state clearly that subscribers can easily opt out of your list whenever they want.

8. **On-demand materials (PDF).** What happens if a prospective client wants to tell someone else about you? The problem with a beautiful Web site is that it usually doesn't look so beautiful when the pages are printed. The way around this is to offer professionally designed PDFs, readable with the free Acrobat Reader. But don't just offer a standard capabilities brochure; we recommend your menu include a how-to guide or tips brochure that includes capabilities information.

9. **Proprietary process.** After specialization, clients look for a specific problem-solving process. You should create this process, name it, trademark it and describe it with reverence on your Web site.

10. **Seminar information.** The best lead generation topic you can employ is the seminar, briefing, workshop and/or round table discussion. Focus on the biggest problems that you solve for clients. Your Web site should prominently list upcoming seminars (to promote attendance) and past seminars (to promote your reputation as an expert).

11. **Privacy policy.** In a confidential business? Then by all means have a clear privacy policy that states you will never share contact information with anyone else.

12. **Legal disclaimer and copyright notice.** For ideas on legal disclaimers, look in the front of any non-fiction business advice book published today. You will see language that says the publisher is not engaged in rendering legal, accounting or other professional service and the information is for educational purposes. And protect your intellectual property—your site content and free resources—by taking advantage of de facto copyright laws. Post a standard copyright notice.

13. **Focus-specific information.** If you are a specialist in a certain industry, like health care or real estate, then there'd better be health care or real estate information throughout the Web site (you don't want to look like a poser or a wannabe).

14. **News releases.** The Internet is the number one research tool for journalists today, so include news releases, fact sheets, firm backgrounders and longer executive biographies in one area.

15. **Public speaking.** List upcoming and past speaking engagements with industry and civic groups. This promotes your reputation as an expert and will also help you garner invitations for future speaking engagements.

16. **Job postings.** Create positive, upbeat descriptions of the stars you attract to your firm (some clients will go here to get a sense of who you really are).

17. **Key employee bios.** Keep these short—say, 50-100 words. Longer bios belong in the news release section.

18. **Client base.** This can be tricky, but it's important. If it is appropriate in your field to list marquee clients, by all means do so. If this is inappropriate, then describe the types of clients you work for in general terms (e.g., "A Fortune-500 Manufacturer of Paper and Consumer Products").

19. **Case studies.** Our focus groups tell us most prospective clients aren't particularly interested in case studies because they believe specific cases don't apply to them and their own problems. A better approach is to take information out of a case study and turn it into a how-to article.

20. **Referral mechanism.** Your Web designer can easily include a feature that makes it easy for someone to refer your Web site to a friend or associate.

21. **Contact mechanism.** The purpose of the Web site is to let prospects check you out and then contact you. Have a device that makes it easy for them to do so.

---

### Deliverable

Working with a professional Web designer (don't succumb to the temptation to let your teenage niece do your Web site for you!), you should create or redesign your site according to guidelines that will maximize trust and minimize user frustration.

Building a site that works takes more than just opening the box and installing FrontPage or Dreamweaver. You'll need a targeted site architecture plan, a user-friendly visual design, a front page with text that reflects your work from Chapters 1-3, and a quick and easy way for users to find your free resources.* You'll also need the capability to gather e-mail addresses and other contact information from interested prospects.

It takes at least 6 weeks to put together a good skeletal Web site. Allow time and energy for the process to take shape.

---

*No, you might not have them yet, but you will soon.*

# Chapter 9 : Conduct Proprietary Research

## What Research Can You Conduct, Collect, Interpret, Or Own?

You need to conduct research that you own. It will come in handy again and again, in print, on the web, and as you talk to clients.

Begin by choosing the three biggest problems your target clients face that your service can solve. What clients want to know most is how they stack up to their competition. Your specific answers from research will command client and media attention.

## And The Survey Said…

Another publicity secret is that the media loves numbers. An easy way to generate news that will get your name out there is to analyze and report statistics. Give the media provocative numbers, and they will give you coverage. This is what we term publicity-generating research. This is how it works. Find a topic that relates to your organization. Commission an opinion survey. Then release the results to the media in a news release that offers your analysis.

Here are some other examples of proprietary research in action, all taken from *USA Today*.

- If you like steamy sex conversations over dinner, you're probably single, according to a survey of 300 men and women conducted by Sfuzzi, a trattoria with locations in New York; Washington, D.C.; Dallas; and Houston.
- The lowly penny has a big following with the public, says a Gallup poll. Of 750 adults asked if the penny should be discontinued, the con-cents-us was clear: 62 percent want to save the single-cent coin. The poll was commissioned by

Americans of Common Cents, a group organized by the zinc industry. Pennies are made mostly of zinc and use less than 3 percent copper.
- A friendly, helpful staff is what 76 percent of patrons want at a fast-food restaurant, according to a Wendy's/Gallup survey of 1,029 fast-food consumers.
- People would rather pay $50 a month for insurance that includes a nursing home benefit than have free coverage without the benefit, says an American Association of Retired Persons study of 1,490 adults.
- Cleveland and Nashville are among the ten cities that will be hot for hotel development in the near future, say hotel real estate consultants Laventhal & Horwath.

## How To Turn Research Into Clients

So you want to build a reputation to win clients? Some of the quickest reputation-building routes are to host seminars, give speeches and write articles. But why should potential clients listen to you?

"Clients today are bombarded with articles, speeches and seminars that contain generalities and do not distinguish the author or presenter from any of his or her competent competitors," says former Harvard Business School professor David Maister. In his highly regarded book *Managing The Professional Service Firm* (a must-read book for all professionals), he discusses how to demonstrate that you have something to offer that your competitors do not.

The answer, says Maister, is a neglected tool: conducting proprietary research on topics of interest to prospective clients. This can be technical or professional in nature, or it also can be general survey research.

Examples of this type of research from professional service and technology service firms are abundant.
- Clients list "creativity" as the most important criterion when selecting a new agency, according to the fourth annual Thomas L. Harris/Impulse Research public relations survey
- Most San Diego employers say they will generally hold the line when it comes to new hiring in the fourth quarter, according to the latest survey by staffing agency Manpower Inc.

## Advantages of Proprietary Research

The information that a potential client most wants to know is, "how does my company compare to others?" There is a hidden fear in the back of the mind of every executive: are we missing out on something? Nobody wants to be behind the learning curve, especially in today's rapidly changing business environment.

Maister, who reportedly charges $15,000 per day to counsel professional service firms on how to improve their business, recommends surveying a cross-section of executives in a given industry. Ask them to prioritize trends they worry about most, list tactics that are of the most use to them, and name devices they use. Then you can report rankings of the most threatening issues and most popular tactics. For enhanced credibility, some firms get client industry associations to co-sponsor and help guide the research.

## Provocative Research Works

By conducting proprietary research, you obtain special information that prospective clients can't find elsewhere. The foundation of client seduction is to give away useful information that demonstrates to clients you have the expertise to help them. Giving away general problem-solving information is good, but it is not good enough. You need to offer specifics, and the more provocatively you can package the results, the better.

Professionals, consultants and technology entrepreneurs can use proprietary research to obtain clients, even during tough economic times. A recent case in point is Enterpulse, an Atlanta-based Web services firm that designs and builds corporate Web sites. Projects can be extremely complex, encompassing both the external and internal Web presence of a company and serving an intricate network of customers, employees, and suppliers.

According to Enterpulse, 2002 was a "now or never" year as the deepening technology recession further eroded sales and prospects. Many of the firm's larger and better-known competitors had gone bankrupt in the previous 12 months. Enterpulse, a mid-sized firm, actually viewed this as an opportunity to become a bigger player and gain market share in its category. But the company needed to make a bold move to raise its visibility, boost sales, and leave its few remaining competitors behind.

To overcome the challenges in communicating with Enterpulse's audiences, the firm commissioned a proprietary research study through Ketchum Public Relations of heavy business Internet users. The survey results would be useful to interest the media in a new story angle on the Internet, and also to give executive information technology (IT) decision-makers compelling data for evaluating their company's Web presence from a user perspective.

The result was 265 qualified U.S. leads for the sales force to pursue, with three of these leads quickly converting to signed contracts. The entire budget was $100,000, including $25,000 in out-of-pocket expenses. More than $1 million in business was generated, which means a return on investment of 1000 percent.

# The Internet Death Penalty

How did they do it? Enterpulse had to overcome two pivotal challenges in communicating with prospective customers:

- Reporters were not particularly interested in writing about the Internet anymore—unless the reporter could unearth a new angle and back it up with examples.
- Making the case for a user-centric Web experience would require strong evidence to convince an analytical, data-oriented audience of IT decision-makers.

With this in mind, they surveyed more than 300 heavy Internet users in the fields of IT, sales/marketing, purchasing, and human resources. The proprietary research results revealed that users overwhelmingly expect Web sites to be user-friendly or they won't return. Enterpulse called this end result the "Internet Death Penalty" and showcased the phrase in press materials and media outreach to attract maximum attention. If you want attention, you need to be provocative.

# How To Publicize Results

But being provocative is only the first step. You also need to be proactive in spreading the results of the research.

Enterpulse CEO Michael Reene published a provocative white paper to alert companies to the fact that they should evaluate their Web presence from a user perspective, or else risk alienating customers. The white paper was featured on the home page of Enterpulse's Web site, www.Enterpulse.com. The firm traded the white paper for e-mail addresses and required interested persons wishing to download a free copy to first input their contact information into an online form.

Enterpulse hired Ketchum to conduct a 30-day media relations campaign. The news release was issued via Business Wire and Internet Wire. Ketchum also contacted national business media, the top 100 daily newspapers, and key trade media in the IT, banking and retail vertical markets. Reporters were provided with a link to the white paper for further information and also offered a detailed analysis of the survey results.

Media interviews were conducted with Reene, who used real-world examples of Web sites relevant to the survey results to support the white paper's premise. A bylined article (based on the news release) was written and placed in several IT-oriented publications.

Media coverage for the survey clearly convinced information technology decision-makers to take a closer look at Enterpulse's thesis—as evidenced by more than 1,000 downloads of the white paper on the Enterpulse Web site by high-profile organizations such as Disney, American Airlines, Princeton University, Hallmark, and Panasonic.

To date, 18 daily newspapers, 60 metro business journals, 20 industry/IT trade publications, and four radio spots have featured Enterpulse's findings. Coverage highlights include *USA Today, Newsbytes, CNET, InfoWorld*, 60+ metro business weeklies around the country, and *Stores Magazine*.

The campaign appears to be spreading virally over time, with additional daily newspapers, Web sites, and other outlets continuing to pick up the survey results from the original wire story and from publications that featured the story.

## Let It Flow

Remember those lectures in science class about the scientific method? Well, it's time to dust off that knowledge. The scientific method is about observing, forming a theory (or hypothesis) and then experimenting to test the results. Here is a flow chart to help with your proprietary research studies.

1. From your experience and observations, pick the three biggest problems you solve for clients and turn each problem into a research topic
↓
2. Ask yourself: "Will this research be relevant to potential clients and trade journal editors?"
↓
3. Review the literature of books, articles and published studies that relate to your research topic
↓
4. Collect data through opinion surveys, focus groups, depth interviews and analysis of case studies
↓
5. Analyze the data to draw conclusions and make recommendations
↓
6. Write a summary report on the findings of your research (this can be as simple as a report or as elaborate as a book)
↓
7. Use the research information in your seminars, speeches, how-to articles, Web site content and publicity

## An Example

A San Diego company that uses this strategy extensively is Harte-Hanks Market Intelligence, a 30-year-old La Jolla-based firm that provides customer relationship management (CRM) services. The company recently conducted a survey of 448 large U.S. corporations to discover how they were implementing CRM programs.

Based on the survey, Harte-Hanks was able to report that one-third of these large corporations have a CRM program in place or will have one in place within the next 12 months. Of those implementing a CRM system, approximately 26 percent are using or building a fully developed in-house solution, while the balance are using a variety of external partners and software packages.

How did Harte-Hanks use this information? The results were published in a white paper that was offered to other large corporations through exclusive executive briefings. The survey content was the basis for speeches at industry conferences and was also used in a series of no-cost, invitation-only, online seminars (also called Webinars) hosted by Harte-Hanks. Finally, the information was used for publicity, both as a general news release on some of the major findings, and as the basis of a how-to article on the top ten successful CRM implementation strategies.

While employing many other marketing strategies, Harte-Hanks Market Intelligence has made proprietary research a key part of its ongoing lead generation system. Overall, the practice has positioned the firm as a primary source of valuable information for clients.

## Harte-Hanks Press Release Examples

# News Release
### FOR IMMEDIATE RELEASE

## HARTE-HANKS STUDY EXAMINES
## 'HIGH-PERFORMANCE' B-TO-B E-MAIL CAMPAIGNS

LA JOLLA, CA – August xx, 2002 – While average business-to-business e-mail response rates are in the 1 to 2 percent range as measured by use of a click-through device, some e-mail campaigns can garner as much as a 25-percent response rate, reports a new study from Harte-Hanks (NYSE:HHS).

What separates the extraordinary e-mail campaigns from the ordinary? That was the purpose of recent Harte-Hanks research, conducted by the company's market intelligence team, which examined 515 permission-based e-mail campaigns to uncover the strategic and creative practices of successful e-mail marketing in 2001 and 2002.

The study primarily focused on business-to-business campaigns in telecom and technology markets that were designed by Harte-Hanks' clients and executed by Harte-

Hanks from August 2001 to May of 2002. Based on this time period, here are click-through response rate averages and ranges, broken out by purpose of campaign:

| Purpose of E-mail Campaign | Average | High | Low |
|---|---|---|---|
| General Marketing | 1.5% | 25.0% | 0.2% |
| Market Research | 4.2% | 21.0% | 0.5% |
| Sales Promotion | 1.8% | 10.3% | 0.1% |
| Offline Seminar Invitation | 0.8% | 7.3% | 0.1% |
| Subscription Offer | 1.8% | 3.8% | 0.1% |
| Online Seminar Invitation | 1.0% | 3.6% | 0.0% |

"While many an e-mail campaign does fail expectations, the potential numbers – as measured by the highs — are still too good to ignore," said Randy Wussler, vice president of product development, market intelligence, Harte-Hanks. "For the same budget, an e-mail campaign can touch twice as many prospects as a traditional direct mail campaign. However, not all e-mail campaigns are created equal."

Based on the 515 e-mail campaigns in the study, Harte-Hanks researchers have compiled a list of the nine "best practices" that separate higher response-generating campaigns from ordinary ones.

## Top Nine High Performance E-mail Best Practices

1. Integrated media messages boost e-mail click-through rates by at least 5 percent. Like any other type of marketing program, the more an e-mail campaign is targeted, the better response it will realize. E-mail marketing should not be viewed in a vacuum. Based on the experience at Harte-Hanks, integrating a telemarketing and direct mail program will boost response rate, from 5 percent to 15 percent, as measured in click-throughs. While one message might suffice, Harte-Hanks has found that an ongoing dialogue using integrated media will lift response with clients and prospects.
2. Personalization is key to high response. Craft messages based on information known about individual recipients, and segments of recipients. While much attention is given to one-to-one marketing, e-mail content crafted for segments perform well, too. For example, content crafted differently for executives in sales, marketing, and senior management will lift response better than the same message sent to all three business titles.
3. Be straightforward in the subject line. The call to action should be the backbone of your subject line, and should include words that describe the offer or reason for action. Such words as "free," "discount," "complimentary," or "this weekend

only" in the subject line lets the creative move response. While marketers often worry about fatigue in their lists, that is not only a matter of frequency but also a function of being misled at the recipient's first encounter with a marketing message. Hiding or cloaking the true intention of a marketing message feeds fatigue and undermines confidence.

4. <u>Clarity of message, offer, and response means is required</u>. Anecdotally, e-mail is opened, scanned and closed at rates faster than direct mail. So it's imperative that every message contain a clear, compelling call to immediate action and provide a transparent response mechanism. The time customers and prospects spend searching for a "reply" button or URL is enough to lose them — thus layout is critical as well as traditional direct marketing discipline and principles.

5. <u>The sender should be a person, not a company</u>. People also are more likely to open e-mail from a person, rather than from a company or some generic server address. Designate a sender.

6. <u>E-mail messages must have a clear opt-out process</u>. Permission is permission, but the choice to take that permission away must be clear to the recipient. The quickest way to earn the wrath of busy prospects and customers is to send an unexpected e-mail with no way for them to opt out. Having a prospect name by way of permission is not an excuse to duck an opt-out option – in fact, it violates Direct Marketing Association and Association for Interactive Marketing ethics guidelines – even for business-to-business and customer e-mails. Never leave a recipient feeling helpless and out of control; the ill will such a campaign generates could be devastating. Make it easy for people to leave gracefully, preferably with a one-click procedure backed up by an 800 number. More and more recipients are noticing which campaigns follow accepted opt-out practices, and they appreciate having the option — even if they don't use it.

7. <u>A response device should be more compelling than a simple link to a home page</u>. In most cases, an e-mail campaign with only a home page link generates higher Web site "hits," but that traffic can get lost after the home page. When using links it is better to have a landing page tailored specifically for the offer in the e-mail message. Still, even a landing page cannot overcome an offer that in itself fails to be compelling.

8. <u>Short and sweet works</u>. Plain text-based e-mails can be very effective if they are targeted, have a compelling call to action and are brief enough to be read quickly. HTML e-mails, if utilized, need to include the same clarity and brevity in organization to elicit response.

9. <u>Saturation points for frequency are low and getting lower</u>. During the research period, it appeared that the optimal frequency for receiving e-mail messages is declining – across all categories. Appropriate use estimates vary widely, should continually be tested, but generally fall within a range of twice a week to twice a month. Err on the side of caution to foster continued good will.

Founded in 1969 and acquired by Harte-Hanks in 1999, the market intelligence team at Harte-Hanks manages the CI Technology Database, a primary source of information on technology purchasing plans and platforms of thousands of businesses in North America, Latin America and Europe. Harte-Hanks, Inc. (NYSE:HHS), San Antonio, TX, is a worldwide, direct and interactive services company that provides end-to-end customer relationship management (CRM) and related marketing service solutions for a host of consumer and business-to-business marketers. Harte-Hanks and its CRM integrated solutions use technology as the enabler to capture, to analyze and to disseminate customer and prospect data at all points of contact. Its customer-centric models allow the company to be the overall solutions provider for driving traffic to a Web site, call/contact center, or brick-and-mortar location. With premier specialized offerings – direct agency capabilities to print on demand, Web page design to e-care, desktop database capabilities to systems integration, personalized direct mail to e-mail, proprietary software products to application service provider (ASP) solutions – Harte-Hanks provides practical implementation of technology and understands the needs of clients and their customers to deliver best-of-breed solutions. Visit the Harte-Hanks Web site at http://www.harte-hanks.com or call (800) 456-9748.

---

News Release

FOR IMMEDIATE RELEASE

## HARTE-HANKS RESEARCH: CRM STATUS REPORT, 2002

*-Harte-Hanks research examines CRM ROI, data access, customer view & systems development approaches across many types of companies-*

LA JOLLA, CA - June 17, 2002 - A new Harte-Hanks (NYSE:HHS) survey of 464 North American companies and their implementation of customer relationship management (CRM) solutions reveals that companies are expanding internal access to customer data and the content of those data is more focused on revenue history than in a similar survey the previous year.

A team of Harte-Hanks researchers conducted interviews in April and May 2002, using a sample of companies drawn from the CI Technology Database of Harte-Hanks. The survey comes one year following a similar survey conducted among 300 companies.

One surprising finding of the CRM survey is the absence of return on investment (ROI) measures at many implementations - 44 percent reported no such measures in 2002, compared to 32 percent in 2001. However, between 37 percent and 52 percent of respondents indicated use of at least one customer-based ROI-type metric in 2002

- metrics such as improved customer service ratings, improved client retention rates, and improved profitability tracking by customer. Reported use of such customer metrics grew by 17 percent between 2001 and 2002.

"The future of CRM investment is dependent on how successful companies document and measure returns today," said Gary Skidmore, president, CRM, Harte-Hanks. "To justify the expense of CRM projects, even in phases, a variety of metrics will be important to ensure continuation of CRM programs, engage users, and determine overall success."

Corporate users of CRM systems and data are extensive, and expanding when compared to the 2001 survey. Marketing departments (both marketing communications, 76 percent, and product marketing, at 62 percent) recorded the largest gains over 2001, while inside sales was the most often cited department for such usage for the second consecutive year, this year at 86 percent.

Among other findings in the CRM Status Report 2002 study:
- Enterprise-wide - External sales forces continue to have more restricted access than inside sales (64 percent have access in 2002) - an indication that legacy sales force automation solutions may not be replaced everywhere a CRM solution is developed. Channel partners have access to customer data in just 16 percent of CRM solutions, but this figure jumps to one in five solutions among those respondents that are planning to implement a CRM solution within the next 12 months.
- A more limited "full" customer view - The array of content provided for in CRM solutions appears to be more focused on client revenue sales/history (68 percent in 2002). Just 19 percent include product purchase history, and 13 percent include tech support and/or customer service history.
- One in five solutions are in-house - Twenty percent of CRM programs are in-house-developed solutions, with no commercial CRM software packages, and very limited, if any, outsourced programming. Among others, 76 percent said they are relying on a commercial CRM package that is being implemented by either in-house or outsourced development resources.
- The data silo challenge - The most significant challenge related to implementing a CRM solution is the presence of data silos within corporations. The survey reveals that 42 percent said integrating different data sources into a single data system is the top challenge, followed by training users to use the solution effectively (37 percent), and participation of different departments within a company (30 percent).
- A corporate initiative - In nearly eight of 10 implementations, CRM is a corporate, rather than a divisional or local initiative. The department most often given the primary responsibility for setting ongoing CRM development and

enhancements priorities is information technology (44 percent), with sales (16 percent), senior management (15 percent), marketing (11 percent) and other departments (14 percent) cited. Among departments charged with developing a CRM management budget, this frequently is an information technology-funded initiative (54 percent). However, among those planning a CRM solution within the next 12 months, senior management is the most oft-cited financer, in 45 percent of the planned solutions.

* With a cross-functional management team - A cross-functional team is the most prevalent method for managing CRM projects, at 42 percent. Thirty-five percent utilize an individual product team, while 23 percent use a designated team inside a specific document.
* Web and wireless access still down the road - The ability to access customer data via wireless and Web media appears to be limited. Fifty-two percent of solutions provide zero users with Web access to CRM data. Just 17 percent enable Web access to more than 75 percent of the corporate user base. Still, 44 percent of those planning a CRM solution within the next 12 months plan to provide 50 percent or more of their corporate users with Web access to customer data, most often an XML-based solution. Wireless access is even more limited, with just 5 percent of respondents giving more than 50 percent or more of their corporate users wireless access to CRM information.

Among respondents, 59 percent of the companies included facilities with 100 or more employees. Eighty-nine percent reported a CRM solution now in place, 6 percent were planning a CRM solution within the next six months, and 5 percent were currently building a CRM solution. In addition, 34 percent surveyed were manufacturers, 29 percent were in the services industry, 15 percent were retailers or wholesalers, 10 percent were financial or insurance companies, and 4 percent were in the transportation or utilities industries. The balance was spread among several other industries.

A full report of the CRM implementations, The CRM Status Report 2002, is available from Harte-Hanks Market Intelligence for $495. Full access to the CRM Database of the CI Technology Database for one year is also available separately. For purchase information, contact (800) 854-8409, ext. 7205.

---

## Homework

Think about the kinds of research you might conduct. Start by looking at your business's records; do you have historical data that might be interesting to others? What secondary research could you mine and reassemble? What kinds of surveys might you use to come up with interesting, publishable data?

## Deliverables

1. A list of studies you can either conduct, create, or manage

2. A target deadline for starting and completing each one

---

# Your Pain Survey

Section 1: Their Demographics. Who's answering? Do they fit your target market profile? Don't go hogwild; this isn't about them as individuals. It's about you and what you need to know.

Job Title: _____

Industry: _____

# of Employees: ___

Section 2: Their Pains. We're trying to find out what they believe and what they're ready to act on, so we can know what to offer folks like them. The first two questions are open-ended, consisting of our BEST GUESSES about what they're frustrated, worried, or concerned about.

1. During the next 12 months, would you say the following are high, medium, or low priorities for you and your company?

| High | Medum | Low | Priorities |
|------|-------|-----|-----------|
|      |       |     | Phrase each possibility as an OUTCOME....i.e., improve morale, increase market penetration, develop new products...make choices 70% things you can help them with, 30% "distractors" or things that everybody, regardless, says is a high priority. |
|      |       |     |           |
|      |       |     |           |
|      |       |     |           |
|      |       |     |           |
|      |       |     |           |
|      |       |     |           |
|      |       |     |           |

2. Do you agree or disagree with each of the following statements?

Here we try to get at the ASSUMPTIONS and BELIEFS that underlie their reasons for buying—or not. What might they believe that would incline them to act faster, or slower? To buy your offerings or not to? Try to phrase these possible beliefs in a non-leading way. Again, a couple old "truisms' never hurt.

| Statement | Agree | Neither Agree nor Disagree | Disagree |
|---|---|---|---|
|  |  |  |  |
|  |  |  |  |
|  |  |  |  |
|  |  |  |  |
|  |  |  |  |
|  |  |  |  |

Section 3: The Big Kahuna: The Open Ended, Heart's Desire, No Holds Barred, Bleeding Pain question.

4. If you were an all-powerful being and you could improve three things about the problems your firm solves, what three things would you choose?

a.

b.

c.

# Chapter 10 : Share the Wealth

## What Insights Can You Give Away For Free?

It's now time to write articles on how clients can solve their biggest problems. These are used on the Web site and in the lead generation efforts. You need to give away information on how to solve problems in general so clients will trust you enough to hire you to solve their specific problems.

## Ghostwriters in Disguise

If writing for you is, as a late *New York Times* sportswriter put it, "easy . . . you just sit down at a typewriter and open a vein," then the tourniquet for you may be a ghostwriter or collaborator.

Getting published is an important variable in the marketing success quotient. Don't let the excuse that you're not a good writer prevent you from earning a byline. A professional can take your rough notes, conversations, and ideas and turn them into something that's polished and well-written.

The essential thing that can never be farmed out, however, is your ability to present quality information and ideas. Your material should spark an "ah-ha" in your readers and ignite them to reach greater heights. If you can prompt someone else to succeed, then you will have succeeded, too.

But great writers don't come cheap. You may be lucky to find a good, hungry writer who is trying to break into magazines or book publishing who is willing to work on speculation. But, typically, you'll get to work that way only once with that author.

Any writer who earns his or her living writing soon discovers that while he or she is writing for nothing, you, the expert, are earning a living in your field. You have an income and a book. The writer has only a byline.

Recognizing that writing is a profession only if he or she can earn a living, a good writer will charge an hourly or project fee to ghostwrite or collaborate. The average hourly rate ranges between $50 and $200. Magazine articles may be written for as little as a few hundred to as much as several thousand dollars. And flat fees for ghostwriting books can reach as high as $5,000 to $8,000.

## Brainstorm Your Article Topics

Here is a proven method for developing the advice that you need.
- Pretend a reporter is interviewing you for this story. What wisdom would you be sure to include? Write it all down.
- After you have brainstormed the list, cut it down to five to twelve best points.
- Write these up as your how-to advice, adding a few words of analysis.

Vagabond Inns, a chain of approximately forty motels in the Western United States, used this strategy to gain national publicity for its 25th anniversary.

Top executives were polled on what secrets they would share with a relative or close friend about staying in hotels. The answers were pulled together in a study called the "Vagabond Inns Insider Report." Several magazines and a wire service columnist published the information and quoted the hotel chain's president as the information source.

This exposure was then parlayed into radio and television interviews. An attractive spokesperson purchased several of the latest travel gadgets so she would have something visual to talk about. A television interview show was so impressed that they taped a series of 3 –5 minute travel tip fillers, which they aired and credited to Vagabond Inns for a whole year. Other than the travel gadget and a little time, the cost of this publicity was minimal.

# Headlines for 'How-to' Articles

*by Joan Stewart*

*Want to write a how-to article but can't come up with a topic? Start by naming the three biggest problems your customers or clients face. You've just come up with three ideas for three different articles. Be sure the topics tie into a service you provide, a product you sell, or a cause or issue you want to promote.*

Once you've chosen a topic, it's time to select a title. Here's a list of possibilities. Simply fill in the blank, depending on what you've decided to write about.

- *A Part-Timer's Tactics for a Full-Timer's _____*
- *A Quiz: Test Your _____ Smarts*
- *Cash in on _____ Trends*
- *Chasing the Right _____*
- *Cool Tools for Today's _____*
- *Common Errors That Kill _____*
- *Discover the 7 Essential Elements That Guarantee _____*
- *Finding the _____ That is Uniquely You*
- *Good News for _____*
- *How to Bounce Back from _____*
- *How to Get Other People to _____*
- *How to Handle _____*
- *How to Make _____ Work for You*
- *How to Make Your _____ Dreams Come True*
- *How to Turn _____ into _____*
- *Mastering the Art of _____*
- *No More _____*
- *Part-Time _____, Full-Time Success*
- *Questions and Answers About _____*
- *Straight Talk from a _____*
- *The Great _____ Dilemma*
- *The Most Beginner-Friendly _____*
- *The Last Word on _____*
- *The Amazing Solution for _____*
- *The Best and Worst Ideas for _____*
- *The Complete Guide to _____*
- *The Worst Mistakes You Can Make When _____*
- *Top 10 _____ Do's and Don'ts*
- *What's HOT and NOT in _____*
- *When Not to _____*
- *Your Must-Know Guide to _____*

- _____ *with Pizzazz!*
- _____ *and Grow Rich*
- _____ *on the Cheap*
- *5 Ways to Get More from Your* _____
- *5 No-Fail Strategies for* _____
- *6 Secrets to Successful* _____
- *7 Ways to Keep Your* _____ *Dreams Alive*
- *7 Ways to Avoid the Most Deadly* _____ *Mistakes*
- *8 Ways to Avoid the Worst* _____ *Mistakes*
- *9 Formulas for Fantastic* _____
- *10 User-Friendly Facts for* _____
- *10 Tips to Jump-Start Your* _____
- *11 Questions You Must Ask When You're* _____
- *12 Tactics to Open Up* _____
- *13 Tips That Will Make a* _____ *Smile*
- *10 Time-Tested Tips for Becoming a* _____
- *25 Quick* _____ *Tips to Use Now*
- *26 Holiday Gifts for* _____

*Copyright 2002 by Joan Stewart. For more free publicity for your professional services business, sign up for "The Publicity Hound's Tips of the Week," an electronic newsletter. Subscribe at www.PublicityHound.com and receive by autoresponder the handy list "89 Reasons to Send a News Release."*

## Homework

Brainstorm at least 6 topics to write about for each of your target audiences. In an ideal world, your topics would fulfill all of the following criteria:
- The material is interesting and valuable to potential clients
- You know a lot about the subject
- The information isn't readily available from your competitors or other sources

Next, get to work creating the resources, either with a ghostwriter or by yourself.

## Deliverables

First drafts of at least six How-To articles (500-1000 words) to post on your Web site. These will also turn into seminar topics, so it pays to research them thoroughly.

# Chapter 11 : Create Your Printable Pieces

## How Can You Produce The Best Possible Visual Impression?

Finally, it's time to think about those print pieces you used to pay big bucks for. You know—the ones that most marketing firms want you to buy by the metric ton.

This time, however, you're going to minimize what you spend on actual printing by using print-on-demand and PDF technology.

Forget thousands of printed brochures. They're a colossal waste of money. They go out of date quickly, they sing your praises and boast rather than building trust, and what's more, they get thrown away. Quickly.

## The Folder

What you need instead is an image folder, one that will not go out of date for a minimum of five years.

The folder itself is the item your potential clients will see—and judge. Therefore, it should be visually appealing, with full color, heavy cardstock, sturdy design, die-cuts for your business cards and no-spill pockets. It should also be a standard size (to fit in a file drawer) and contain as few words as possible.

There are several techniques that will ensure the folder has a long and useful shelf life.
* No local phone number
* No address
* 800 number

- Web site address
- Use color
- Few words
- Pockets for inserts

## The Contents

Next comes the contents: Adaptable documents that you can place in your folder, customizing for the occasion. You may choose up to three target markets, and need materials to adapt to each one. This allows you to project an image of a specialist with a specific process for each target client base.

Typical contents:
- Firm resume
- How-to information
- White papers
- Guidebooks
- Short bios
- Reprints of articles
- Seminar invitations

## The PDF

Finally, it's time to create that brochure—but you aren't going to pay to have it printed. Instead, create an electronic version that can be read by anyone with an e-mail address and free Adobe Acrobat software. You'll of course hire a graphic artist to do the same careful, professional layout that you normally would have to do for a print job. But when the artist is finished and you've approved the draft, you have your final product already. No printing time, no printing costs, no delays. Instant gratification.

You can post the brochure on your Web site, e-mail it to clients and even use your own laser printer to create print-on-demand versions for those Internet-averse potential clients.

---

### Homework

Get your marketing print materials in order. Set deadlines and meet them.

#### Deliverables

1. Your Image Folder
2. Folder Contents for each target audience
3. A PDF brochure

---

# Chapter 12 : Book Your Suspects

## Where Will Your Prospects Come From? How Will You Manage Them?

Before they can be prospects, they've got to be suspects.

The world of potential buyers is like a miner's sieve; you're panning for the gold nuggets. And to find them, you've got to go through a whole lot of sand.
The first step is to find the names, addresses and phone numbers of people who you suspect might become a client. This database will become the cornerstone of your marketing outreach efforts.

Research shows that 50 percent of the success of lead-generation efforts depend on this first step.

Once you've obtained all this information, it's time to organize and manage it; you have options. You might need to explore the capabilities of such software as MS Excel, MS Access, ACT and/or Goldmine.

There are many outlets from which you may purchase or obtain lists.
- Trade associations and professional groups
- National vendors like InfoUSA, Dun & Bradstreet, and Harte-Hanks
- Strategic partners who sell complementary services
- Industry shows
- …and on and on…

The list must be maintained if it's going to do you any good, and one person in your organization should update it as mail gets returned or phone calls with corrective information are received.

Finally, as much as it hurts when you want to ramp up quickly, you'll need to build your e-mail list from the ground up. Unsolicited e-mail is called "spam," and as its density increases all over the internet, so does the level of hostility and frustration about it—in legislators and, maybe more importantly, in the minds of the very prospects you're trying to woo and win. Never send a "blast" e-mail to people you haven't met, or who haven't somehow given you permission to send them e-mail. You'll do more harm than good.

---

## Homework

Think about the kinds of people you want to reach—the people who are good potential clients. What is their industry, position, company size, geographic location?

## Deliverable

Obtain a list of these people.
Load it into a robust contact management system.
Get ready to roll.

---

# Chapter 13 : Become A Journalist

## How Can You Get Your Name Into Print?

You need to get published by submitting query letters with article ideas to trade journals that your prospective clients read. The sad truth about trade journal articles is that editors reject 90 percent for being too promotional and not including hard numbers.

It may be time to hire that ghostwriter.

For specifics about how to complete this step, read on.

## Magazines And Newspapers

So where should your how-to article appear? The answer is probably waiting for you in your in-basket. You likely already subscribe to the leading trade journals for the industries of your target clientele.

If not, you can use a resource that professional public relations people turn to every day: Bacon's Directories, which list publication and editor information for almost every media outlet there is. Your local library will have copies if you don't have the budget to purchase them (as of this writing, a complete set of *Bacon's* directories, covering newspapers, internet sites, television, radio, and magazines, ran a cool $1,200).

How do you use *Bacon's?* Start by building a simple spreadsheet or database of contact information for publications you think your story might fit in, including the right editor, if one is listed. Then start sending queries, using whatever format the editor has listed as a preferred contact method.

# The Bylined Article

Here's some good news. Want your article to appear in *The Wall Street Journal?* That's not very likely, because that publication is almost entirely written by staff journalists. But for most trade journals, only about half of the articles are written by staff journalists. The other half are written by practitioners in the field.

This is a deal where everyone wins. The publication wins because it gets quality articles it does not have to pay for. The readers win because they get expert advice from in-the-know professionals and consultants. And you win because you get some of the most potent publicity you could ever hope for to build awareness for your firm.

However, not all trade journals and industry publications accept bylined articles (a byline is the journalists term for having your name appear with the title of the article, as in by your name). Flip through the pages and see if you see articles written by practitioners. If you are in doubt, read the blurb that appears at the end of the article. This should contain the person's name, title, company and how to reach them (either a Web site or e-mail address). Find that and you have found opportunity.

But what if you don't subscribe to the publications? Then do what all good public relations people do. You need to obtain a copy of *Bacon's Publicity Checker* from Bacon's Publishing Co. of Chicago. This is the publication that lists, by subject and alphabetically, the thousands of trade journal magazines and newsletters. There is a wealth of information about each publication. In addition to listing how many people read the publication, *Bacon's* also indicates if the publication accepts bylined articles.

# Study The Trade Journal

Editors will accept only articles that provide information and omit the promotional language. This is not an advertisement that you control. If you violate this basic principle, the editor will reject your story. The good news and the bad news is that editors probably reject 90 percent of the how-to article ideas that are submitted; bad news if you make it too promotional, good news (less competition for you) if you write it like a staff writer.

Be sure to visit the publication's Web site. Many will include a section on guidelines for writers. This will give you valuable information about how to submit ideas, article length, style, format and other advice. Other publications will send you a sample issue and writer's guidelines upon request.

How do you find out who is the right person at the trade journal to send your article idea? Pick up the phone and call. Research indicates that turnover among editors may be as high as 1 percent per week. If the directory you have is six months old, it may be 25 percent out of date.

# A Sample Query Abstract

Eating The Microsoft.NET Elephant

*One Byte At A Time*

The much-hyped rollout of Microsoft's .NET platform has some executives with IT responsibilities wondering what the new framework can do for them. At the outset, it appears that broad adoption of .NET in the marketplace isn't a question of if, so much as when. Business leaders know there's a lot at stake, and they're wondering how to deal right now with the inevitable migration to web-based XML services.

What may not be apparent at the outset is that migration to .NET can be achieved through evolution, not revolution. Starting immediately, there are many small-scale, practical implementations of the new technology that CIO's and IT Managers can leverage. Change needn't happen suddenly and massively; smaller scale projects affecting existing tools may, in fact, allow information managers to gain experience and demystify the migration process.

For most companies in a struggling economy, full and immediate .NET migration is simply not an option. Companies can, however, roll out Microsoft. NET incrementally and economically to extend the capabilities of their existing IT systems.

Four immediate applications that can reap concrete benefits from the .NET framework are:

- BizTalk Server 2000,
- Microsoft SQL Server 2000,
- ASP.NET
- XML Web Services

This article will use case studies to illustrate real-world applications of .NET to existing tools, focusing specifically on how to choose, plan, and complete small-scale .NET integration projects.

Writer: Bill Edmett, Jr. , Partner, Practice Management

As co-founder of SCG, Bill has been working with the company since it's inception in 1993. Bill is responsible for all managed projects at SCG requiring high-end, mission critical Application Development and Integration services. He has been instrumental in defining SOLUTIONSMethod, a proprietary framework used by SCG for ensuring predictability and increasing productivity in the software development process. Since forming SCG, Bill has delivered many large-scale database solutions for companies such as Harcourt Brace, Kaiser Permanente and Sony. Prior to forming SCG, Bill worked as an independent, full-time billable consultant for Safeskin Corporation, Kelco and Career Guidance Foundation.

# Send A Query Letter

Before investing time and money in writing a how-to article, pitch the idea to the trade editor first. This can be done with a short, compelling letter or e-mail. Once you have his or her go-ahead, you can interview your customer.

Once you've honed your angle, you're ready to approach an editor. Don't pick up the phone and call. Just as if you were selling any other product, you need to write a convincing, professional proposal. But don't worry, it doesn't need to be lengthy; in fact, the shorter the better.

Editors want ideas submitted in the form of a one-page letter called a query. They don't want to see the entire manuscript. And you're wasting your time by writing the entire article before you know if you have a salable idea or the specific slant an editor may want.

Query letters do three primary things. They:
* Demonstrate that you have a fresh angle on an important topic.
* Show that you have the ability to write an article in a way that will interest the magazine's readers.
* Prove that you are the expert to write it.

It's important that your letter not just whisper your idea in a boring business letter style. It must trumpet it in a way that will be music to the ears of an editor whose in-basket is deluged with proposals from professional writers, public relations agencies and others who want to see their names in print. Your first paragraph—the lead to your letter—should capture the imagination of the editor by painting a scenario with a real-life anecdote, offering a startling statistic, posing an intriguing question, or turning a phrase in such a way that it makes the editor want to know more.

# Submit Your Article

Congratulations, the editor says the publication will consider publishing your article. Now what? When you write your article, here is something to ponder. Most trade editors are always looking for interesting case histories. Most want solid numbers to back up the story, but are willing to accept percentages (e.g., sales increased 44 percent over the previous year, expenses were cut by 56 percent, two out of three customers are now experiencing gains).

Perhaps the most difficult part of obtaining trade journal publicity may be selling your best customers on the idea of agreeing to be interviewed. The time commitment on their part is probably three to five hours during the next four weeks. They will want to be assured they won't be giving away any trade secrets. Probably about 1 in 4 will agree to share the information, data and procedures that you need.

Before you submit your article, be sure to spell check and fact check the document. Having someone else read and edit your article also is a must. Finally be sure the word count matches the guidelines of the publication. If everything checks out, send that article. Most publications want the article sent via e-mail, so they can download the information directly into their computers.

## Four Other Ways To Get Your Name In Print

Not ready for the full-fledged how-to article? There are other ways to see your name and Web site address in print. These were suggested by Martin Hill, former editor of the *San Diego Business Journal*.

- **Write a letter to the editor.** According to Hill, these are among the most well-read items in a newspaper or trade journal, but editors don't receive as many letters as they would like. "Write a letter commenting on a particular business issue, a news event or a story that appeared in the publication," advises Hill. Letters should be brief and include your name, address and daytime phone number (in case they need to check a fact).

- **Write an opinion column.** Hill recommends you choose a topic you feel strongly about and argue your case in less than 800 words. But be careful. Columns that promote a specific company or product will not be used. Sometimes it is a good idea to send the editor a brief e-mail with a thumbnail of what you intend to write.

- **Suggest a story about a business trend you've spotted recently.** Send a brief e-mail to the editor and they will consider it when they make story assignments. Give your credentials on why you would be a good resource to be interviewed for the article.

- **Suggest a story idea to one of the columnists in the publication.** Typically columnists won't promote a specific product or service. But they do need spokespeople to round out a story. Always ask if they would publish your Web site address, but if they can't you understand. If you don't ask, you don't get.

---

### Homework

Start converting your free resources and proprietary research into query letters that you send to the most relevant press.

### Deliverables

A list of target media
A list of articles you could write
At least one query letter per month, distributed to your target media list.

---

# Chapter 14 : Hold Small-Scale Seminars

## How To Turn Seminars Into Increased Revenue

Generating new client leads through seminars is a proven strategy. But some professional service firms and technology service companies are frustrated with a lack of turnout for the seminars they host. By following some best-practice strategies, you can dramatically increase seminar and event attendance.

First, scrutinize your proposed topic by asking yourself some hard questions. If prospective clients attend this seminar, what beneficial information will they receive? Is this information that my competition either cannot, or does not, offer? Is this information a strong enough pull to justify them spending their precious time with us?

Next, examine how you spread the word. Do you have the right mailing list? If so, maybe direct mail alone is not sufficient to deliver enough prospects to your next seminar. A key to attracting high-level executives is to reinforce direct mail messages with phone calls. These calls also can provide valuable feedback on how prospects view the seminar topic and subject matter.

Perhaps time and distance are keeping you apart. If you serve clients that are located throughout the country (or perhaps, the world), there is an online alternative to face-to-face seminars.

An online seminar (or Webinar) is an interactive, real-time way to hold online meetings and conferences. By eliminating the barriers of time and space, Webinars enable you to share information with thousands of customers or partners anywhere in the world, through a standard Web browser. With a Webinar you can conduct seminars, training, product demonstrations and collaborative meetings, thereby significantly lowering the cost of communications and reaching people whom otherwise would not participate because they are unable to travel to your meeting.

## How To Make It Work

You may have a great idea for an event to attract potential clients. But it's quite another to pull it off successfully. The myriad of small details involved can make or break an event. Here are some recommendations to maximize the success of your next lead generation seminar.

1.  Develop a checklist and timeline for pre/post seminar activities
2.  Decide if this will be a free briefing or an event that you will charge for (there is a time and place for both)
3.  Use informal research to pretest topics to make sure the one you choose has the most appeal to your target audience
4.  Make sure the letters or invitations you use reflect a first-class image for your firm
5.  Confirm registrations 48 hours before the event by e-mail
6.  Deliver seminar content that is of real value to clients, not a thinly disguised sales pitch for your services
7.  After the seminar, make it easy for the potential client to contact you in the future by sending a thank you e-mail/letter with phone number and Web address
8.  Conduct an organized follow up five to ten days after the seminar or event in an effort to start a dialogue with potential clients
9.  Measure how much the seminars cost and how much revenue was ultimately generated to calculate your return on investment (ROI)

## Getting The Word Out

Event letters or invitations should be mailed or e-mailed approximately four weeks prior to the event. Give registrants the option to call the 800 number, fax, e-mail or utilize the on-line event registration application on the Internet to register for an event. When possible, it is helpful to provide detailed information on your invitations for the location of your event and an overview of what will be covered. Here are some business-to-business seminar scheduling guidelines:

*   No seminars on weekends
*   Avoid Monday and Friday
*   Avoid seminars in a holiday week (Fourth of July)

- Check for conflicting industry events

The best months to hold a seminar in rank order are:

1. March
2. October
3. April
4. September
5. November
6. January
7. February
8. June
9. May
10. July
11. August
12. December

Telemarketing calls can increase registrations five percent beyond the registration rate from direct mail. Calling is conducted one to three weeks prior to the event. Many seminar experts recommend three call attempts per contact with voice messages on the first and third attempts.

Typically, only 50 percent of those who say they will attend a free seminar actually attend. To minimize no-shows, confirmation e-mails are another option to consider. Send an e-mail confirmation 48 hours prior to the event. The e-mail confirmation will act as a reminder of the event and provide them date, time, location and directions. E-mail confirmations can greatly increase the attendance rate at the event.

## Final Thoughts On Details

You might ask yourself, are all these details that important?

Remember, the purpose of seminars is to introduce you to potential clients and provide evidence on what it would be like to do business with you. Clients will form many preliminary impressions about you through the seminars. Know this: you are being judged based upon whether you are organized, thorough and willing to invest in the relationship by providing valuable information.

## After The Event

After the event is completed, it is always recommended that you follow-up with the event registrants.

**Follow-up letters -** Even if someone didn't attend the event, it is a good idea to send a letter to these potential new customers and give them the opportunity to visit your event Web site or call in to the appropriate toll free phone line and get additional product information. It is recommended that the Thank You/Regret Letter go out within five business days of the actual event.

**Post-event calls -** Each event response should receive a post-event outbound phone call. If a customer takes the time and potential money to learn more about a product, it makes good business sense to outbound call all the event attendees and walk them through a lead qualification script. Outbound telephone qualifying gives you the ability to score the event attendees and to customize your post-event follow-up to match the customers' buying cycle.

**Post-event surveys -** Based on experience, Harte-Hanks recommends that the sales cycle should be checked for accuracy. They have done numerous post-event surveys with their customers' event leads and found out that the sales process hasn't met the customer expectation. In a lot of cases, they have taken those customers and re-introduced them to the sales process. It is Harte-Hanks' recommendation that these types of surveys are performed four to six weeks after the actual event. You should create "Did You Buy" outbound scripts that get to the bottom of customer satisfaction.

**Response analysis -** Preparing a response analysis report is vital. This report should include all attendee answers to evaluation form questions, which generally include budget, authority, need and time frame.

**List performance -** You should have direct mail experts analyze how different lists perform vs. expectations. From this you can also develop other criteria for selecting lists based on attendee/lead demographics. For example, there may be 100 attendees at a seminar, but only 5-10 turn into qualified leads. Rather than pulling the same list using the same criteria moving forward, model those 5-10 qualified leads and pull other lists using that criteria. At future seminars, you may only have 20-30 attendees, but those attendees are higher quality and you will have realized a significant cost savings by targeting them.

**Registered/attended analysis -** Perform seminar analysis to determine the effectiveness of each event. Basic seminar analysis would include registered/attended analysis. This is the type of item that is a baseline percentage to use to measure success of a seminar. There are techniques that can be used to increase this percentage significantly, including confirmation calling, and confirmation e-mails.

# Example Seminar Registration Form

Name
Position
Firm Name
Nature of Firm
Total # of
employees
Phone
E-mail

Part 1: Marketing Issues

1. My firm and I could be more effective and would attract more clients if we could deal more effectively with the following challenges:
*(Check all those that apply and circle your #1 challenge)*

☐ We're not in front of enough new prospects to keep the pipeline filled
☐ We're not attracting the right kind of qualified new prospect
☐ Not enough prospective clients are aware of our firm
☐ Other firms get more exposure in the media than we do
☐ Other firms get more exposure from speaking engagements than we do
☐ We lack publications that demonstrate our credibility to prospects
☐ Networking and referrals are no longer producing enough prospects
☐ OTHER *(please specify)*

2. If the challenges above were overcome, our annual billings could increase by:
☐ Less than $50,000
☐ $50,000-$250,000
☐ $250,000-$500,000
☐ $500,000-$1,000,000
☐ More than $1,000,000

3. As a ballpark guess, the average lifetime billings from a typical client are:
☐ Less than $10,000
☐ $10,000-$100,000
☐ $100,000-$500,000
☐ $500,000-$1,000,000
☐ More than $1,000,000

Part 2: Survey of Interest

On a scale of 1-10 (top priority), my level of interest in generating more leads is:

1☐ 2☐ 3☐ 4☐ 5☐ 6☐ 7☐ 8☐ 9☐ 10☐

Level of interest in a phone call to discuss this further:

☐ No, I have no interest.

☐ No, but put me on an e-mail list for tips and newsletters

☐ Yes, I would like to meet. Call me on:

## Make It Virtual: Teleclasses

Another emerging trend is to offer teleclasses, also known as telephone seminars or teleseminars.

"The best clients are those who seek you out because they have already heard of you," says Steven Van Yoder, author of the excellent book *Get Slightly Famous,* and an advocate of teleclasses. "Having heard you speak, people feel they know you personally, and are more confident about hiring you."

The advantages are abundant. You don't have to be personally present to give a talk that reaches your target market. Online chats and teleconferences, using your own or others' telephone lines, can help you reach a lot of people eager to hear your message.

Teleclasses are a great way for businesses to provide information to prospects, clients, and customers all over the world, with minimal cost and effort. Unlike seminars and other meetings, they eliminate the need to travel. Both hosts and participants can attend from their offices, their favorite easy chair at home, or even by mobile phone while on vacation. Teleclasses make it easy to connect to prospects all over the world.

*Get Slightly Famous* provides a systematic approach for getting consistent media attention, using speaking engagements to cultivate a market, leveraging the Internet to its full potential and becoming a center of influence within your industry. A part of Van Yoder's chapter on speaking highlights why teleclasses are popular with professionals and consultants.

Teleclasses are, in essence, virtual classrooms created with an automated conference call system called a "bridge line." Students register for a teleclass, receive the virtual-classroom telephone number, and call it at the appointed hour to get connected to the host and other attendees in a format that is part lecture, part interactive classroom.

Even one teleclass can help you expand your potential market. You don't have to be physically present, but can reach the entire world.

"I participated in one class recently (with 500 attendees) that helped me sell books in the U.S., U.K. and Australia and even landed me an interview on an Australian radio show (the host just happened to be on the call)," adds Van Yoder. "I'm also using teleclasses as teasers for paid programs and as an opportunity to give people a taste of me, my book and services in a value-oriented, no-risk manner." (For more information, see his Web site at www.getslightlyfamous.com).

The book is filled with several practical teleclass examples. For instance, business coach and teleclass leader Michael Losier took his first teleclass three years ago and was impressed with the potential for this type of meeting. Because it was so convenient and so much fun, he decided to try running one himself, and set up a teleclass about exhibiting at trade shows. "I had 60 students in my first class, which was very profitable, and many later hired me as a consultant," says Losier.

Since then, teleclasses have helped Losier expand his market, and gotten him a stream of international clients. "After just six months of teaching teleclasses I was able to leave my desk job. I ended up writing two books on my teleclass courses, thanks in part to the feedback my students gave me. I also became a teleclass trainer to leaders across the globe."

The book also shows how teleclasses offer an alternative to live presentations and seminars that doesn't put added stress on people's already jam-packed schedules. Teleclasses enable you to bring together 10, 20 or 100 people to listen to you talk about your business for an hour, allowing you to engage them and display your mastery.

Some teleclasses typically meet once a week for three to four weeks, with each meeting lasting 55 minutes. This gives students a chance to absorb a topic in bite-sized pieces, like a short college course, with time in between classes to apply what they've learned.

Many businesses are also offering free teleclasses (or one free initial teleclass) as an affordable way to connect to groups of targeted prospects and attract new business.

As in any class, the quality and effectiveness of the experience depends on getting people to participate and interact. And by their very nature, teleclasses are more interactive. They make it easier to participate, because in a roomful of strangers, many attendees are too shy to speak up.

That's why teleclasses often experience increased participation among attendees. They are highly interactive, more like tele-discussions, which make it easier to share and be heard, to ask questions and get answers (they also, of course, make it easy for the very shy to just sit and listen as if they were hiding in the back row of a classroom). "In teleclasses, there's no worry about body language, or turning red when you speak," says one teleclass leader chronicled in the book. "Participants are more free to engage in the teleclass."

Perhaps that is the biggest advantage of all for the professional and consultant who wants to gain more business. The business logic is this: the more engaged the prospect, the more likely they are to hire you and spread the good news around about your expertise.

# Chapter 15 : Write A Book

## What Do You Know? How Can You Put It Into A Book?

You may be intimidated when you hear "Write a book!" You probably think it's a huge, hairy, audacious, arduous task—something you might get to in retirement, but certainly not a project you're willing to tackle right now.

You might want to think again.

Nothing will boost your credibility, your newsworthiness, your reputation, your potential for publicity, or your profile like having your name as an author or co-author on the cover of a specialized book for your target market. Nothing. These days, you don't necessarily need a publisher to become a published author. With the advent of on-demand self-publishing companies, it's possible to assemble your specialized niche expertise in one impressive place and not blow the entire marketing budget on the endeavor.

The least you'll need to write a book is an outline, a title, and a good ghostwriter. The most you'll need is a few months in which you can generate the text yourself. No matter how you get the manuscript written, though, it's well worth your investment. Think about it: How many times in the last 120 days have you thrown away a brochure?

Now…how many times in the same period have you thrown away a *book?*

Books are almost sacred. Books are special. Books—even small books—get kept. Books are gifts from you to your prospect. Don't give them a slick, expensive brochure. Instead, give them a piece of your mind—literally.

# Chapter 16 : Give How-To Speeches

## Where Can You Establish Your Reputation As An Expert?

Publication grows naturally into public speaking. Here you share your expertise from the platform by giving how-to speeches to groups that your prospective clients attend.

The trick, as always, is to offer valuable information, not a commercial for your firm (a real audience turn-off that works against you). The two main venues are association meetings and college extended study programs (and they love guest speakers).

## 17 Ways To Find An Audience

First, let's acknowledge a universal truth. Nobody likes public speaking. At least, not at first. Standing in front of a group of strangers can be nerve-wracking. Luckily, there's a cure, and it's simple: Practice, practice, practice.

Few things make as much client seduction sense as speaking. Your prospects get to see you and hear you sharing expertise without any risk. Speeches are a perfect opportunity to be seen, heard, and most importantly, remembered.

Securing speaking engagements, however, is not as easy as throwing your name into a hat. You have to prove yourself and your credentials: A strong business track record, a unique message worth hearing, and compelling speaking skills.

Here are 17 tactics you can use to get speaking engagements—and deliver memorable speeches.

1.  If you need to learn how to speak, join Toastmasters. Not only is such a group likely to attract other success-oriented professionals, it's also a great, low-threat way to pick up practical pointers, watch other dynamic speakers in action, and begin to get used to the idea of speaking to groups.

2.  Start with family, friends and colleagues. Just ask. As with other things in life, our circle of influence is often more connected to what we want than we might realize. Want to talk to local hiring managers at technology firms? Ask around and you might be surprised how many people in your network can suggest groups you might approach.

3.  Package yourself. Write a one-page letter that explains who you are, what your background is, and three to five topics on which you are prepared to speak. Make this your standard "speech pitch." Also make sure you have a one-paragraph biography, introductory paragraphs for each speech, and a pre-written introduction (to YOU) available for the people who book you.

4.  Prepare a 30-second commercial for your speaking. Condense what you have to offer to an audience as much as possible: "I'm Joann Blough, and I'm an expert on Floral Arranging. I speak to more than thirty groups a year on unique floral approaches to wedding decor, leveraging in-season blooms for special event purchasing, and expanding the floral decorative market into corporate offices." Use this "elevator speech" when you network and socialize.

5.  Buy a copy of a local directory of clubs and organizations. Most major cities have directories of active groups that use speakers. In Southern California, SourceBooksUSA, headquartered in San Diego (www.sourcebooksusa.com) produces a guide that's updated quarterly. This kind of directory can be an invaluable resource when you're sending out letters offering your speaking services.

6.  Identify groups by consulting the Encyclopedia of Associations.

7.  Study trade journals.

8.  Ask others who would know.

9.  Staff and committee members can tell you about procedures for selecting speakers.

10. Contact university extension instructors and offer to be a guest lecturer. Be sure to use handouts that are printed on your stationery that includes your phone number and Web address. Extension students seem to be more motivated, better educated and more attuned to forming alliances than the average person in the industry.

11. You can be paid to speak as a university extension instructor.

12. Speak for groups like the Learning Annex.

13. Offer to do in-house training for corporations.

14. Tie in to your local chamber of commerce.

15. Approach conferences that are scheduled to take place in your area, or in your industry. Send them your speaker's introduction kit and topic list. Follow up with a phone call.

16. After a speech, offer to hold a small roundtable discussion for those who are interested. This can be later in the day, at a coffee break or over cocktails, and is a great way to solidify your position as a trustworthy expert, and to extend the impact and influence of what you've said to the larger group.

17. Consider going pro. The National Speakers Association (NSA) offers practice and networking for experts who get paid to speak. Once you're proficient at talking about your expertise, check them out and watch the opportunities expand.

---

## Homework

Identify a list of potential organizations, meetings, trade shows, and associations where you can deliver speeches to likely prospects. Harvest interesting topics from earlier Chapters and get in contact with the people who arrange speakers for those meetings. Offer to share your research, your information, or your how-to advice at their next meeting.

---

# Chapter 17 : Plant A Referral Tree

## With Whom Can I Build Ongoing, Mutually Beneficial Relationships?

Different databases do different things. In this Chapter, you'll create a special database of up to 100 opinion leaders that you know and would greet you warmly when you contact them. If you want referrals, you need to give referrals.

For a professional, consultant or entrepreneur trying to build a business, referrals are too important to leave to chance. You need a proactive process that will encourage referrals on a continuing basis. Here are the highlights of two excellent books that are required reading for those who want more referrals.

In *The Referral of a Lifetime*, author Tim Templeton emphasizes the importance of "putting the relationship first." For Templeton, gaining more referrals is as easy as A-B-C. He offers precise instruction on creating a database of your best 250 contacts.

- The A list is your best 10 percent of contacts. These are the people who are most likely to refer business to you. You should physically mail something to these people every month. "They are the easiest to identify as they will jump off your list and say hello to you like an old friend," says Templeton.
- The B list is the 20 percent of contacts who you think can champion your cause and refer you, if you educate them about how you work. These people should receive something from you every other month, for a total of six mailings a year. Tell them to let you know if you can help them in any way, and promise to treat referrals as well as you treat them.

- The C list is the remaining 70 percent of your "best contacts." You may not be sure about whether they're really a referral source, but still, you want to communicate with them. You mail something to these people every three months, for a total of four mailings a year.
- After the C's, there's everybody else: Call them D's. These people are the remaining names in your database. Maybe you need to keep their phone numbers, but you don't choose to work with them. They receive no ongoing communications.

For some professionals just starting out, it will be a stretch to come up with 250 contacts. IT firms and more established businesses, on the other hand, might have to cull down a huge list to get to 250.

Once the prioritization is finished, you will need to choose a basic contact manager program (like *Act!, Goldmine, Microsoft Outlook or salesforce.com*). The only requirement, beyond what you already know and are comfortable with, is that you can use the program to set up custom fields and categorize your contacts as A, B, C or D.

| A's | B's | C's |
|---|---|---|
| Jan | Jan | Jan |
| Feb | | |
| March | March | |
| April | | April |
| May | May | |
| June | | |
| July | July | July |
| Aug | | |
| Sept | Sept | |
| Oct | | October |
| Nov | Nov. | |
| Dec | | |

A—mail to monthly, give them something fun and creative
B—mail to bimonthly, send an article or useful tip
C—mail to quarterly, send a card

But some people may be wondering, how do you find these people in the first place? What is the best way to network with people at business functions, like Chamber of Commerce mixers or association luncheons?

Bob Burg, author of the book *Endless Referrals*, says "All things being equal, people will do business with, *and refer business to*, people they know, like and trust."

One key to quickly establishing this type of connection is showing interest in other people by asking them questions. Burg has developed a series of questions to ask people at networking events that are not sales-oriented in any way. These are fun questions to ask and fun questions to answer.

While you will never need or have time to ask all of his questions during a conversation, Burg maintains it is good to have an arsenal to choose from. Here are his 10 questions:

1. *How did you get your start in the widget business?*
2. *What do you enjoy most about your profession?*
3. *What separates your company from the competition?*
4. *What advice would you give someone just starting out in the widget business?*
5. *What one thing would you do with your business if you knew you couldn't fail?*
6. *What significant changes have you seen take place in your profession through the years?*
7. *What do you see as the coming trends in the widget business?*
8. *Describe the strangest or funniest incident you've experienced in your business.*
9. *What ways have you found to be the most effective for promoting your business?*
10. *What one sentence would you like people to use in describing the way you do business?*

Burg's next question is the one that is key in getting the person to feel as if they know, like and trust you. "How can I know if someone I'm talking to would be a good prospect for you?"

That final question shows you are concerned about them. You may be the only person who asked them this question during a first conversation.

Then, wrap up the conversation in another surprising fashion: Instead of offering them your business card, ask for one of theirs. Follow up by sending them a thank you in the mail containing your business card.

These techniques might just land you in their database of preferred contacts. Each month you should systematically water your referral tree, and it will bear fruit.

## 100 Friends

_____

_____

_____

_____

_____

## 10 Advocates

## Homework

Identify your list of 100 and your list of 10. Brainstorm ways to reach out and touch them all each month.

## Deliverable

Populate your contact manager with the two new lists. Commit a specific amount of time each month to contacting the people on your referral tree, and then follow through.

# Chapter 18 : Join Community/Civic/Trade Groups

## How Can You Get More By Giving More?

Be a joiner, but be selective about where you decide to donate time as a member of a committee or board. You should be genuinely interested in the cause and the group should include potential clients and referral sources.

Use your status as a board or committee member to seek advice from key players inside and outside the organization. Here are some recommendations to accomplish all that and more.

- Strive to join groups in which you are one of the few representatives from your profession or corporate rank, rather than organizations comprised solely of professional colleagues.
- Let someone convince you to join the group. Use him or her as an ally to become a leader of the group, but avoid assignments that require maximum work with minimum reward.
- It is more important to attend the social hour than the meeting itself.
- Do your homework before joining a group. Begin by forming a linkage with the key staff person.
- Joining the membership committee is a smart way to gain the favorable attention of the group's power structure.
- Seek out high-visibility assignments, such as ad-hoc committees that report to the board of directors.

- When you discover that an organization doesn't exist in an area where you want to form alliances, take advantage of a golden opportunity and form such a group.

---

## Homework

Start by listing the organizations you'd genuinely like to serve in an active capacity. What are your interests? What charitable or civic activities do you enjoy?

Next, narrow your list down. Which of those groups are likely to attract the kinds of people who would be potential clients?

Commit to attending several meetings of one or two finalist organizations before you join for good. The dynamics of each group are different, and you should be able to gauge how beneficial your involvement might be within the first couple of months.

---

# Chapter 19 : Keep Networking

## What Are The Three Best Groups Or Functions Where You Could Network?

Next, circulate to percolate. The key is to make networking at business functions a game that you score a goal for each business card you obtain (not give away).

## Don't Join Any Club That Would Have You As A Member

It pays to be a joiner. To advance your career or build clientele, it's essential to take part in professional groups. Work toward becoming a leader of one or more clubs; do that by joining the right committee. Do some homework before volunteering. Determine the chairpersons and members of various committees, then join those comprised of people with whom you want to form linkages. Committees give you a chance to show off your stuff (not just swap business cards), plus an opportunity to get to know all of the members.

## Top Five Networking Don'ts

Everyone wants to get those million-dollar leads. But, the truth is unless you devote the time to develop a network you're never going to get them. Building relationships is the key, but that takes time.

For professionals, consultants and entrepreneurs, becoming involved with business associations are one of the quickest ways to meet people. According to one expert, the trick is to visit organizations where your potential clients are, where there are people like you (for support and information) and, at least, one that offers some type of training. "Unfortunately, networking is like eating a healthy diet," says career-management expert Annette Richmond. "We all know we need to increase our contacts if we want to be successful. But, we'd rather not walk into a room of 50 people we don't know. I know I should eat a nutritious diet if I want to stay healthy. So every morning I eat Oatmeal with Soymilk for breakfast. Now that oatmeal is OK, but I'd rather have a jelly donut. "

Richmond says it is the same with networking. You know you should go to the association's monthly dinner. But, you'd rather go home and catch a little TV. Watching TV seems more appealing than pumping hands with a bunch of strangers.

But, it doesn't have to be that way. Once you become more comfortable meeting people the easier it will be to go to events. And as your networking efforts begin to bear fruit, you'll become more excited when you have the opportunity to connect with new people.

Richmond is founder of career-intelligence.com, an online career resource, and principal of the Richmond Consulting Group, which provides guidance, workshops and seminars on a wide range of communication, leadership and other work-related issues. In her workshops Richmond doesn't promise to turn people into networking machines who look forward to attending every seminar and meeting. However, mastering a few techniques can help you change your attitude and become a better connector.

Here are Richmond's top five networking don'ts:

### 1.Don't Get Caught Off Guard
Often we're uncomfortable with the idea of meeting new people because we think we have nothing to say. The solution is to plan ahead: have three topics you're prepared to talk about. Look for interesting tidbits in the local newspaper, on a morning talk show, even in an entertainment magazine. Go online and find out more about the speaker. "Don't worry about being profound," says Richmond. "Just be able to carry on a conversation."

### 2.Don't Be a Space Invader
At networking events "in your face" is not a good thing. Have you ever met someone who moves in to greet you and then stays there? The scenario goes like this: someone moves into your space, you move back, they move closer, you move back. Soon you are engaged in a dance around the floor. To avoid being a space invader, Richmond advises to always maintain your distance. While preferred distance varies by culture, Americans typically consider three to four feet their "personal space". Don't go there.

### 3.Don't Work the Room

When you're having a conversation give the other person your complete attention. Don't glance around the room to see who else is there. Or look at your watch. Or gaze out the window. "People know if they have your attention," says Richmond. "They also can tell when you're looking for someone more important to talk to."

### 4.Don't Be Pushy

"Sometimes it's good to be aggressive and sometimes it's good to wait till you're asked," advises Richmond. "When it comes to giving out your business cards go for the latter." We've all met pushy people: You've barely met them, yet already their business card has found its way into your hand.

Business cards are a wonderful tool. They are a great way to help people remember you and keep in touch after you've made a connection. The operative phrase is "after you've made a connection."

What can you do if they don't ask? Ask them. Most people will reciprocate when you ask for their card. If they don't, ask them if you may give them your card. At least you've given them the courtesy of asking.

### 5.Don't Be Forgettable

Try to avoid answering, "What do you do?" with your title (Senior VP Business Development) or occupation (lawyer). Instead create a 30-second "elevator" speech that explains what you do.

"Let's say you sell real estate. Lot's of people do," says Richmond. " So be sure to include a something that makes you stand out." Maybe you are an expert at finding homes for growing families? Maybe you find homes in a hurry? Pick whatever makes you unique. That's what makes you memorable. Spend some time creating your elevator speech and rehearse it until it comes naturally. Being confident and relaxed helps to make you memorable.

---

## Homework

Repeat the process you went through in Chapter 18, only this time, target professional groups rather than charities and civic organizations.

---

# Chapter 20 : Send (E-)Newsletters

## What News Can Your Prospects Use?

You need to send out news that prospects can use. This can be done in traditional printed format or in the more cost-effective electronic e-mail version (actually, each one has a time and a place).

- *It's newsletter to me*. Newsletters are great, *if they are newsworthy*. Newsletters are poor marketing investments if they are not read. Just throwing in the company news releases from the past quarter is not a good idea. Instead, stimulate your editorial thinking and identify topics with high reader interest.
- *To get their attention, try grabbing them*. How good are the lead paragraphs of your articles? The most important paragraph in a newsletter article is the first one. If you want to increase newsletter readership, you need articles with attention-grabbing leads. Here are a dozen lead paragraphs that grab attention:
  - alliteration
  - anonymous person (not their real name)
  - epigram or famous quotation
  - historical anecdote
  - humor/pun
  - paint-the-picture description
  - philosophical statement
  - poem/song lyrics
  - pop culture allusion
  - question/do you
  - quote
  - round-up of illustrations

- *Here's a tip.* Include stories with tips, trends and tactics. Newsletter readers always welcome tips on product selection, installation, maintenance, repair and troubleshooting.

- *News you can use.* Another winner for newsletter readers is a how-to article. Similar to a tips story, a how-to article includes more detailed information and instructions. You can explain how to use the product, how to select the right model or how to maximize performance.

---

## Homework

Plan a newsletter to reach out and touch people who have already raised their hand. Decide the following: How frequently will you send it? To whom? Will it be electronic or printed? What will you do to ensure that the information inside is valuable and useful to your audience? Who will write it? Send it? Update the mailing lists?

## Deliverable

Your newsletter plan.

---

# Chapter 21 : Get Publicity

## How Can News Drive Traffic To Your Web Site?

You must continually get the name of the firm out to the media. Research shows that publicity is the number one reason prospective clients will visit your Web site, so each piece of publicity should be designed to promote the Web site address.

You do not need psychic powers to predict the news. Certain stories appear with regularity. Sex, money and health are the three topics that are always in style. If you can provide new information on these subjects, the media will always welcome your input.

Other topics come in and out of style. Just like there are fashions in clothes and cars, there are fashions in news. To be a quoted authority, think not only news topic but also what is in style for this news season. Here is a month-by-month list of news topics. Newspapers, magazines, television, and radio are looking for fresh spins on these ageless news pegs.

- January      Fitness, prediction, Super Bowl
- February     Romance
- March        Spring training
- April        Baseball
- May          Moms
- June         Weddings, graduations, dads
- July         Vacations, Fourth of July
- August       Hot weather
- September    Back to school, football
- October      World Series, Halloween

- November      Elections, Thanksgiving
- December      Holidays, year-end wrap-ups

Another predictable aspect of media coverage is the anniversary story. For example, major news events are re-examined after intervals of one, ten, twenty, twenty-five and thirty years. Not only does history repeat itself, so does the news.

---

## Homework

Brainstorm ideas for press releases, events, and publicity that you could implement during the next year. Think of ways to tie in stories to predictable holidays and events. Come up with at least one idea per month, and then find a way to follow through.

## Deliverable

A list of story or event ideas

---

# Chapter 22 : Send Direct Mail

## How Can You Pique Interest Through the U.S. Mail?

The best use of direct mail is to offer some form of free consultation or how-to literature. Your success will depend on testing various lists and offers until you find the one that clicks.

- *What, me worry about the writing?* As we figure it, more than half of the success of your business-to-business (B2B) offers depend on great strategic writing. Direct mail pioneer Ed Mayer is credited with coining the 40-40-20 rule. Simply put, 40 percent of your success will be determined by how well you define the audience (the list). Another 40 percent will be determined by how the audience responds to how it perceives your product, service and offer (writing the offer). Another 20 percent is determined by the creative package, which includes artwork and the copywriting (again writing).
- *You're on my list.* Varying direct mail lists can change response rates from plus or minus 100 to 1,000 percent. (A favorite story of ours is about the upscale business that had an envelope come back stamped "cannot deliver without inmate registration number").
- *Make me an offer.* In B2B direct mail it is crucial to have an offer that is quickly and easily understood. Offers are really a combination of the product and service, the price and payment terms, incentives and specific conditions. The best offer you can make is to invite prospects to seminars where you will share valuable information, such as your proprietary research.
- *Permission granted.* With e-mail marketing you can benefit from a level of selling that is unavailable in the direct mail world. The key is the opt-in approach, in which prospects give their permission for you to contact them with offers.

- *Build a permissible e-mail list* of prospects who would like to receive more information about your product or service.
- *Diligently collect e-mail addresses* during all your lead-generating efforts, including trade shows and telemarketing.
- *Embed links* to a merchandising Web site in your e-mails, giving you an instantaneous fulfillment package online.
- *Avoid e-mail clutter by customizing.* By extracting specific information from your customer database, you have the ability to construct personalized messages for each reader.

---

## Homework

Brainstorm the most cost-effective offers you could mail to prospects. Carefully evaluate the potential for ROI before committing to any one campaign. What can you offer? What lists will you buy? What is the potential value of a new customer procured this way? The cost?

---

# Chapter 23 : Advertise

## What Trade Journal Or Directory Is Perfect For Your Target Audience?

Advertising has to be highly targeted to be cost-effective. The trick, then, is to find appropriate directories and trade publications in which to advertise the firm name, the promise, and the Web site address. This is usually done with the water drip torture method: small, continual drops of information, endlessly repeated, can have more impact than one large expenditure.

---

### Homework

Go to the library, your own mailbox, and local media sources to determine the best possible vehicles for you to advertise in. Draw up a list—then get reps on the phone. Look at the numbers and make judgments carefully, placing frequency and long-term exposure before size and splash.

### Deliverable

You'll need copy. Short copy. Concise copy. Copy that points a reader to your Web site, tells them you've got free information there, and then quietly fades away.

---

# Chapter 24 : Create Informational Media

## What Information Do They Need At Their Fingertips?

When you send or give away guidebooks, CD-ROMs, DVDs, or other useful media, potential clients will keep them on file. When's the last time you actually kept a brochure around, just in case you needed it?

The trick is to spend as little money as possible to get prospects to raise their hands to request the media. You can offer it to your e-mail list, send a postcard, announce availability at a speech, write about the offer in your column, or send a letter.

Better than sending the guidebooks to everyone on your list. Use the guidebook as a promotional offer in your direct mail. Some professionals buy books and offer an author's book through direct mail.

---

### Homework

Gather together and look hard at all of the how-to information and proprietary research you've already created. Is there a guidebook there? A CD-Rom? If not, what would it take to get there?

### Deliverable

Develop a long-term plan to create informational media. Start with your clients' pain and work from there. What would be most valuable for them? What would they keep in their filing drawer? Expect to spend considerable time in the planning and production of your informational media, and make sure its quality, look, and usability all inspire trust.

---

# Chapter 25 : Hire Phone Callers

## Do They Know They Need You? Would A Phone Call Help?

When everything else has been exhausted, it's a fine idea to use the phone to reach out to prospects. But there are a few caveats.

The professional himself or herself should never carry on the cold call campaign, because the professional's time is too valuable to spend it sifting through "Nos" looking for the "Yesses" that are out there.

You may, however, obtain good results by hiring a full- or part-time business development person who can reach out to cold leads with polish and professionalism.

Following up seminar and special event invitations is an excellent strategy to reach out to more prospects.

---

### Homework

Evaluate whether it might be effective for you to initiate an outbound calling program.

---

# Chapter 26 : Track And Refine Your System

## How Will You Know What's Working?

If you want to see return on investment (ROI), you'll need to track each lead generation program to refine your system.

To quote the scientist Lord Kelvin, "If what you know cannot be measured your knowledge is of a meager and unsatisfactory kind."

For a seminar program, here is what you might want to track on a spreadsheet:
- Number of exposures to your message
- Responses generated
- Response rate
- Seminar attendees
- Attend rate
- Leads generated
- Number of Sales
- Sales volume
- Average sales
- One-time costs
- Implementation costs
- Cost per exposure
- Cost per response
- Cost per attendee
- Cost per lead
- Cost per sale

# Homework

Assign a person to "own" your tracking system and give them the list above to build a spreadsheet or database that will track, in-house, the results of each of your lead generation efforts. Tailor the recordkeeping to your own business, of course. And commit to reviewing your ROI at least quarterly, making whatever course adjustments you think are necessary to raise ROI.

# Deliverable

■Assignment of tracking ownership

■Database or spreadsheet

■Scheduled reviews of ROI

# Appendix A : Further Reading

*1001 Ways to Market Your Services—Even if You Hate to Sell* by Rick Crandall (Contemporary Books, 1998). This specific guide to marketing and sales methods provides 1001 real examples of professional marketing. It is filled with short, interesting examples, highlighted by pictures, tip boxes, and an "Action Agenda" at the end of each chapter with ideas and reminders to summarize.

*Become a Recognized Authority In Your Field In 60 Days or Less!* by Robert Bly (Alpha, 2002). This book is about how to quickly become the preeminent, in-demand guru in your field and gives many steps on how to promote and market your knowledge and skills.

*Creating New Clients—Marketing and Selling Professional Services* by Kevin Walker, Cliff Ferguson, and Paul Denvir (Continuum, 2000). This book outlines the skills required for maximum success in professional service firms, noting that selling themselves is based on chemistry, trust and an expected long-term business relationship. Their advice is based on the PACE Pipeline model, meaning that the opportunities for future business flow are generated by accumulated efforts and activities.

*Managing the Professional Service Firm* by David Maister (Free Press Paperbacks, 1997). In this general book on firm management, Maister states that all professional service firms have the same mission statement, essentially, "service, satisfaction, and success." His book gives advice on dealing with clients, management, partnerships and managing practices with multi-locations.

*Marketing Your Consulting and Professional Services, 3rd Edition* by Dick Connor and Jeff Davidson (John Wiley & Sons, 1997, $39.95). The book outlines four important "how-tos to ensure success:

- How to ensure satisfaction
- How to make client-centered marketing a natural activity
- How to make the most of your relationships
- How to work from your comfort zone

*Million Dollar Consulting—The Professional's Guide to Growing a Practice* by Alan Weiss (McGraw-Hill, 1998). This guide urges the reader to push the envelope and go beyond their normal practices. It helps to target, land, and keep powerful clients, as well as establishes the firm's image and intensifies its profile. Weiss also gives tips on bases for fees and using new technology as a tool of business.

*Rainmaking—The Professional's Guide to Attracting New Clients* by Ford Harding (Adams Media Corp, 1994). This is the self-help guide for a professional wanting to enhance his sales and marketing skills. It is divided into three parts: obtaining leads, advancing and closing the sale, and building the right marketing strategy for you. The book uses checklists and appendices to highlight the written and visual material, including how to develop and customize a marketing strategy, network effectively, write articles to draw clients, and use direct mail to attract new clients.

# Appendix B: Works Consulted

Aaker, D. A. (1995). *Strategic market management.* New York: John Wiley & Sons, Inc.

Abraham, J. (2001). *Getting everything you can out of all you've got.* New York: St. Martin's Griffin.

Barlow, C. P. (1992). Generating organizational trust and credibility. *Journal of Soil and Water Conservation, 47,* 236.

Beckwith, H. (1997). *Selling the invisible: A field guide to modern marketing.* New York: Warner Books.

Bermont, H. (1991). *How to become a successful consultant in your own field.* Prima Publishing.

Bly, R. W. (2001). *Become a recognized authority in your field – In 60 days or less!* Alpha Books.

Bly, R. W. (1998). *Business to business direct marketing.* Chicago: NTC Business Books.

Boylan, M. A. (1997). *The power to get in.* New York: St. Martin's Griffin.

Broom, G. M. & Dozier, D. M. (1990). *Using research in public relations: Applications to program management.* Englewood Cliffs, New Jersey: Prentice Hall.

Broom, G. B. & Harris, J. H. (1999). A conceptual framework for measuring organizational credibility. Paper presented at Educators Academy Conference of the Public Relations Society of America, University of Maryland, June, 1999.

Burg, B. (1999). *Endless referrals.* New York: McGraw-Hill.

Burgoon, J. K., Birk, T., & Pfau, M. (1990). Nonverbal behaviors, persuasion, and credibility. *Human Communication Research, 17,* 140-169.

Carter, R. F. (1965). Communication and affective relations. *Journalism Quarterly, 42,* 203-212.

Center, A. H. & Jackson, P. (1995). *Public relations practices: Managerial case studies & problems.* Upper Saddle River, NJ: Prentice Hall.

Chartprasert, D. (1993). How bureaucratic writing style affects source credibility. *Journalism Quarterly*, 30, 150-159.Chew, F., & Kim, S. (1994). Using concept mapping to go beyond the source credibility model in assessing celebrity-message congruence. Paper presented to the Theory and Methodology Division of the Association for Education in Journalism and Mass Communication Annual Conference, Atlanta, August, 1994.

Connor, D. & Davidson, J. (1997). *Marketing your consulting and professional services*. New York: John Wiley & Sons, Inc.

Crandall, R. (1998). *1001 Ways to market your services: Even if you hate to sell*. McGraw-Hill Trade.

Cutlip, S. M., Center, A. H. & Broom, G. M. (1994). *Effective public relations*. Englewood Cliffs, New Jersey: Prentice Hall.

DeVries, H. & Gage, D. (1991). *Self-marketing secrets: Winning by making your name known*. San Diego: Pfeiffer & Co.

Franklin, R. A. (1996). *The consultant's guide to publicity: How to make a name for yourself by promoting your expertise*. New York: John Wiley & Sons, Inc.

Gaziano, C. (1988). How credible is the credibility crisis? *Journalism Quarterly*, 65, 267-278.

Gaziano, C., & McGrath, K. (1985, Aug.). Measuring the concept of media credibility. Paper presented to the Association for Education in Journalism and Mass Communications, Memphis, TN.

Gerber, M. E. (1995). *The e-myth revisited*. New York: Harper Business.

Godin, S. (1999). *Permission marketing: Turning strangers into friends, and friends into customers*. New York: Simon & Schuster.

Haley, E. (1996). Exploring the construct of organization as source: Consumers' understandings of organizational sponsorship of advocacy advertising. *Journalism of Advertising*, 25 (2), 19-35.

Hamilton, M., & Stewart, B. L. (1993). Extending an information processing model of language intensity effects. *Communication Quarterly*, 41, 231-246.

Hammond, S. L. (1986, May). Health advertising: The credibility of organizational sources. Paper presented at the annual meeting of the International Communication Association, Health Communication Division, Chicago, IL.

Harding, F., (1994). *Rain making: The professional's guide to attracting new clients*. Adams Media Co.

Hart, C. W. (1998). *Extraordinary guarantees: Achieving breakthrough gains in quality & customer satisfaction*. Brookline, MA: Spire Group.

Hayden, C. J. (1999). *Get clients now: a 28-day marketing program for professionals and consultants*. New York: AMACOM.

Herbig, P., Milewicz, J., & Golden, J. (1994). A model of reputation building and destruction. *Journal of Business Research*, 31, 23-31.

Higgins, R. B., & Bannister, B. D. (1992). How corporate communication of strategy affects share price. *Long Range Planning*, 25 (3), 27-35.

Higgins, R. B., & Diffenbach, J. (1989). Strategic credibility—The basis of a strong share price. *Long Range Planning*, 22, 10-18.

Hoffman, K. D. & Bateson, J. E. G. (2001). *Essentials of services marketing: Concepts, strategies, & cases*. Harcourt College Publishers.

Hopkins, C. C. (1998) *My life in advertising & Scientific advertising*. Chicago: NTC Business Books.

Hovland, C. I., & Weiss, W. (1951). The influence of source credibility on communication effectiveness. *Public Opinion Quarterly*, 15, 635-650.

Hovland, C. I., Janis, I. L., & Kelley, H. H. (1953). *Communication and persuasion*. New Haven, CT: Yale University Press.

Judd, L. R. (1989). Credibility, public relations and social responsibility. *Public Relations Review*, 15, 34-40.

Judd, L. R. (1995). An approach to ethics in the information age. *Public Relations Review*, 21, 35-45.

Kern, R. M. (2001). *S.U.R.E.- Fire: Direct response marketing*. New York: McGraw-Hill.

Kohl, S. (2000). *Getting attention, leading-edge lessons for publicity and marketing*. Butterworth-Heinemann.

Leathers, D. G. (1992). *Successful nonverbal communication: Principles and applications*. New York: Macmillan.

LeBlanc, M. (2000). *Growing your business!* Edina, Minnesota: Beaver's Pond Press.

Levinson, J., Gallagher, B. & Wilson, O. R. (1992). *Guerrilla selling*. Mariner Books.

Lorsch, J. W., Tierney, T. J. (2002). *Aligning the stars*. Boston: Harvard Business School Press.

Lovelock, C. (2001). *Services marketing: People, technology, strategy*. Upper Saddle River, New Jersey: Prentice Hall.

Lovelock, C., Wright, L. (1999). *Principles of service marketing and management*. Upper Saddle River, New Jersey: Prentice Hall.

Maister, D. H. (1997). Managing the professional service firm. New York: Simon & Schuster.

Maister, D. H. (2000). *True professionalism: The courage to care about your people, your clients, and your career*. New York: Touchstone Books.

Maister, D. H., Green, C. H., Galford, R. M. (2000) *The trusted advisor*. New York: The Free Press.

McCroskey, J. C. (1966). Scales for the measurement of ethos. *Communication Monographs*, 33, 65-72.

McCroskey, J. C. (1997). *An introduction to rhetorical communication* (3rd ed.). Boston: Allyn and Bacon.

McCroskey, J. C. , & Jensen, T. A. (1975). Image of mass media news sources. *Journal of Broadcasting*, 19, 169-180.

McCroskey, J. C., & Mehrley, R. S. (1969). The effects of disorganization and nonfluency on attitude change and source credibility. *Speech Monographs*, 36, 13-21.

Montoya, P. (2002). *The brand called you.* Personal Branding Press.

Noelle-Newmann, E. (1980). Mass media and social change in developed societies. In G. C. Wilhoit and H. de Bock (eds.), *Mass communication review yearbook*, 1 (pp. 657-678). Beverly Hills, CA: Sage.

Ogilvy, D. (1985) *Ogilvy on advertising.* New York: Vintage Books.

Ohanian, R. (1990). Construction and validation of a scale to measure celebrity endorsers' perceived expertise, trustworthiness, and attractiveness. *Journal of Advertising*, 19, 39-52.

Powell, F. C., & Wanzenried, J. W. (1991). Perceptual changes in source credibility: Repeated tests using two candidates during a political campaign. *Perceptual and Motor Skills*, 73, 1107-1114.

Powell, F. C., & Wanzenried, J. W. (1992). An empirical test of the Leathers Personal Credibility Scale: Panel responses to the Clinton candidacy. *Perceptual and Motor Skills*, 75, 1255-1261.

Powell, F. C., & Wanzenried, J. W. (1995). Do current measures of dimensions of source credibility produce stable outcomes in replicated tests? *Perceptual and Motor Skills*, 81, 675-687.

Putman, A. O. (1990). *Marketing your services: A step-by-step guide for small businesses and professionals.* New York: John Wiley & Sons, Inc.

Rackham, N. (1988). *Spin selling.* New York: McGraw-Hill Book Company.

Salwen, M. B. (1987). Credibility of a newspaper health story: The influence of source and source intent. Paper presented at the Association for Education in Journalism and Mass Communication, Mass Communication and Society Division, San Antonio, Texas, August 1-4.

Sandler, D. H. (1999). *You can't teach a kid to ride a bike at a seminar.* Stevenson, MD: Bay Head Publishing, Inc.

Scheff, T. J. (1967). Toward a sociological model of consensus. *American Sociological Review*, 32 (1), 32-46.

Severin, W. J., & Tankard, J. W. (1992). *Communication theories: Origins, methods and uses in the media.* New York: Longman.

Shenson, H. L. & Wilson, J. R. (1993). *138 Quick ideas to get more clients.* New York: John Wiley & Sons, Inc.

Spoelstra, J. (2001). *Marketing outrageously: How to increase your revenue by staggering amounts!* Austin: Bard Press.

Tokheim, C. L., Wanzenried, J. W., & Powell, F. C. (1990). Cigarette smoking: Effect on perceptions of source credibility. *Psychological Reports*, 66, 1388-1390.

Walker, K., Ferguson, C. & Denvir, P. (1998). *Creating new clients: Marketing and selling professional services.* New York: Continuum.

Wanzenried, J. W., & Powell, F. C. (1993). Source credibility and dimensional stability: A test of the Leathers Personal Credibility Scale using perceptions of three presidential candidates. *Perceptions and Motor Skills*, 77, 403-406.

Weiss, A. (2002). *Million dollar consulting: The professional's guide to growing a practice.* McGraw-Hill Trade.

Young, D. (1996). *Building your company's good name.* New York: American Management Association.

# About The Authors

Henry DeVries, MBA is a newspaper columnist, adjunct professor at the University of California, San Diego and group research director of the New Client Marketing Institute (www.newclientmarketing.com). A graduate of the Leading Professional Services Program at the Harvard Business School, he has spent 25 years researching specific lead generation strategies that can launch ordinary professionals into extraordinary success.

Denise Bryson, MA coordinated local marketing for the Chicago office of global consulting giant Bain & Company before moving to the book publishing division of the American Medical Association. Immediately before joining the New Client Marketing Institute as vice president of client services, she wrote and produced MBA course content for online education pioneer Cardean University.

Printed in the United States
76848LV00004B/42

9 781418 444808